GOODBYE GOD?

Goodbye God?
An illustrated exploration of science vs religion

First published in 2015 by
New Internationalist Publications Ltd
The Old Music Hall
106-108 Cowley Road
Oxford OX4 1JE, UK
newint.org

© Sean Michael Wilson

Artwork by Hunt Emerson

The right of Sean Michael Wilson to be identified as the author of this work has been asserted in accordance with the Copyright, Designs and Patents Act 1998.

Printed by PBtisk s.t.o., Czech Republic, who hold environmental accreditation ISO 14001.

MIX
Paper from
responsible sources
FSC
www.fsc.org
FSC® C004378

British Library Cataloguing-in-Publication Data
A catalogue record for this book is available from the British Library.
Library of Congress Cataloging-in-Publication Data.
A catalog record for this book is available from the Library of Congress.

ISBN 978-1-78026-226-0

GOODBYE GOD?

Sean Michael Wilson & Hunt Emerson

An illustrated exploration of
SCIENCE VS RELIGION

Foreword
by Lawrence M Krauss

It is a privilege to be able to pen a few words to support this volume. As parents, we owe it to our children to provide them with the best tools we can to thrive into adulthood. As teachers, we owe it to children to encourage them to openly question, and also to provide them with the tools to try to answer their questions. If we can do these things, we have hope that the next generation will live in a better world.

Some people have argued that because a significant number of people doubt the results of evolutionary biology we should teach alternatives in the public schools. But, consider the fact that, when polled in a survey by the National Science Foundation, 50 per cent of US adults claim the statement 'The earth orbits the sun and takes a year to do it' is false! Does that mean that we should teach both an earth-centered solar system in addition to a sun-centered solar system in schools, so as not to offend anyone's sensibilities?

Surely not! As I am quoted as saying in this book, the purpose of education is not to validate ignorance, but to overcome it! If a significant fraction of the US public doesn't know the earth orbits the sun, we need to do a better job of teaching about this in schools. Similarly, if a significant fraction of the US public doubts the results of evolutionary biology, for whatever reason, it means we have to do a better job teaching about it in school, rather than pay lip service to alternative ideas that have long been discredited.

And don't be fooled – ideas like Intelligent Design have no scientific currency. They are so vague as to be untestable in most cases and, in the rare cases where proponents have made testable claims, these have been empirically wrong.

Evolution is one of the best-tested scientific ideas around. Scientists don't use it because we like it. We use it because it works, from understanding our own origins, to helping to develop new drugs.

Withholding knowledge from children because we don't like its implications does them a disservice. Most religions suffer from the same weakness: they provide answers before asking questions. Claims of absolute truth are made without justification, and science teaches that there are in general no such absolute truths – as we explore deeper, reality often becomes more nuanced, forcing us to extend notions that seem appropriate on human scales.

If our society is to function at its best, no notions should be sacred, beyond questioning, including religious notions. That is why we need books like

Goodbye God? – to help expose both religious and scientific nonsense that can get in the way of sound thinking, and to help produce a healthier and happier world with public policies that properly address the challenges of the 21st century.

Lawrence M Krauss is Foundation Professor and Director of the Origins Project at Arizona State University. A theoretical physicist, he is also the author of bestselling books, including *The Physics of Star Trek* and *A Universe from Nothing*.

Part 1

Evolution and Creationism

THIS BOOK IS ABOUT SOME *VERY BIG QUESTIONS*... ABOUT THINGS WHICH ATTRACT A GREAT DEAL OF POWERFUL EMOTION AND PROVOKE INTENSE DEBATE... ABOUT THE METHOD BY WHICH WE *LIVE OUR LIVES* AND *JUDGE OUR WORLD*.

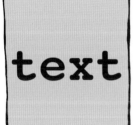 +

WELL, YES. BUT WHAT IS A *COMIC BOOK* OR A *GRAPHIC NOVEL* OR A *MANGA*? IT'S JUST THE COMBINATION OF *TEXT* AND *IMAGES*.

FOR WHAT REASON WOULD SUCH A COMBINATION NOT BE ABLE TO TACKLE SO-CALLED 'SERIOUS' SUBJECTS?

smiling despite the pain

THERE IS NO REASON. SO *LET'S GET STUCK IN...*

IN PART ONE WE'LL BE INVESTIGATING VARIOUS ASPECTS OF THE CONFLICT BETWEEN *SCIENCE AND RELIGION*.

HOW, FOR INSTANCE, THE ISSUE OF *CREATIONISM* VERSUS *EVOLUTION* IS BEING PLAYED OUT IN EDUCATION...

CREATIONISM v EVOLUTION

FIRST OF ALL IT'S USEFUL TO CONSIDER WHAT IS *CREATIONISM?* AND WHAT IS THE *THEORY OF EVOLUTION* THAT IT APPEARS TO BE IN CONFLICT WITH?

THIS IS WHAT THE *US NATIONAL CENTER FOR SCIENCE EDUCATION* SAYS ABOUT CREATIONISM...

'CREATIONISM REFERS TO THE RELIGIOUS BELIEF IN A SUPERNATURAL DEITY OR FORCE THAT INTERVENES, OR HAS INTERVENED, DIRECTLY IN THE PHYSICAL WORLD. THERE ARE MANY VARIETIES OF CREATIONIST BELIEF.'

'SOME FORMS OF CREATIONISM HOLD THAT NATURAL BIOLOGICAL PROCESSES CANNOT ACCOUNT FOR THE HISTORY, DIVERSITY AND COMPLEXITY OF LIFE ON EARTH. SUCH "ANTI-EVOLUTION" CREATIONISTS HAVE BEEN LEADING OPPOSITION TO THE TEACHING OF EVOLUTION SINCE THE 1920S.'

NOW, WE COULD BE *FLIPPANT* AND SUMMARIZE CREATIONISM BY JUST SAYING *THIS...*

BUT LET'S BE FAIR AND LOOK AT IT A BIT MORE CLOSELY.

CREATIONISM
Because it's a lot easier to read one book than a bunch of hard ones.

BEFORE THAT, THOUGH, WE SHOULD SAY SOMETHING ABOUT THE OTHER SIDE: THE THEORY OF EVOLUTION. ACCORDING TO THE *NEW SCIENTIST* MAGAZINE...

Charles Darwin

"EVOLUTION HAS SEVERAL FACETS. ONE OF THESE IS THE THEORY THAT ALL LIVING SPECIES ARE THE MODIFIED DESCENDANTS OF EARLIER SPECIES, AND THAT WE ALL SHARE A COMMON ANCESTOR..."

"...ALL SPECIES ARE THEREFORE RELATED VIA A VAST TREE OF LIFE."

EVOLUTION IS DRIVEN BY A PROCESS OF NATURAL SELECTION OR THE 'SURVIVAL OF THE FITTEST.'

OF COURSE, THIS IMAGE IS A BIT SILLY. BUT, MORE SERIOUSLY, DARWIN ARGUED THAT, WHILE ALL INDIVIDUALS STRUGGLE TO SURVIVE ON LIMITED RESOURCES, SOME HAVE SMALL DIFFERENCES THAT GIVE THEM THAT LITTLE BIT GREATER CHANCE OF SURVIVING, COMPARED WITH THOSE THAT DON'T HAVE THOSE TRAITS.

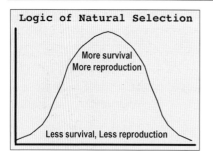

SO INDIVIDUALS WITH THOSE TRAITS HAVE A BETTER EVOLUTIONARY 'FITNESS'. AND THOSE USEFUL TRAITS BECOME MORE COMMON AS THEIR OFFSPRING INHERIT THEM AND SO ARE ALSO MORE LIKELY TO SURVIVE. MORE *SURVIVAL* AND MORE *REPRODUCTION!*

SO NATURAL SELECTION EVENTUALLY PRODUCES A POPULATION, OF WHATEVER TYPE OF ANIMAL, THAT IS WELL SUITED TO ITS ENVIRONMENT. FOR EXAMPLE, DARWIN OBSERVED FINCHES ON THE GALAPAGOS ISLANDS THAT HAD DEVELOPED DIFFERENT TYPES OF BEAKS SUITED TO CERTAIN TYPES OF FOOD – SOME HAD THIN EXTENDED BEAKS FOR ROOTING OUT GRUBS, OTHERS HAD LARGE CLAW-LIKE BEAKS FOR GRINDING DOWN FRUIT AND BUDS.

ANIMALS LIKE THESE FINCHES HAVE ADAPTED. THIS MEANS THE ABILITY OF A SPECIES TO SURVIVE IN A SPECIFIC NICHE HAS BEEN ENHANCED BECAUSE OF CHANGES IN ITS FORM OR ITS BEHAVIOR, VIA NATURAL SELECTION.

BUT IT IS NOT JUST THAT TRAITS IN PARTICULAR ANIMALS GIVE THEM A SURVIVAL ADVANTAGE; THERE'S ALSO THE IDEA OF 'SEXUAL SELECTION', WHICH WAS INTRODUCED BY DARWIN IN 1859.

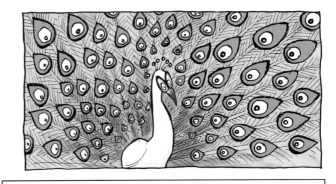

Mr. Macho of 1840 –
Charles Darwin!

CHICKS DIG THE TATTOO.

Image by Denny Liu

WELL, *WHY NOT* FIND SMART GUYS LIKE HIM SEXUALLY ATTRACTIVE? *INTELLIGENCE* MAY BE ONE OF THE MAJOR HERITABLE COMPONENTS OF BIOLOGICAL FITNESS.

WHICH DOESN'T MEAN *WORKING OUT IN THE GYM*, IT MEANS *'THE ABILITY TO BOTH SURVIVE AND REPRODUCE'.*

THOUGH, SOME RESEARCHERS SEEM TO DOUBT THAT. THEY SAY THAT INTELLIGENCE IS NOT AN *'HONEST SIGNAL'* OF FITNESS – MEANING SOMETHING THAT MAKES GREATER BIOLOGICAL FITNESS APPARENT IN AN HONEST WAY.

PARKING HERE IS **FREE!** NO CHARGE!

HONEST!

BUT THERE ARE PLENTY OF THINGS WHICH ARE CLEARLY AN *HONEST SIGNAL*, AND THOSE TRAITS ARE SEXUALLY SELECTED... SUCH AS A MALE FIDDLER CRAB'S *OVERGROWN CLAW.*

OR A *SPRINGBOK'S LEAP* THAT SHOWS ITS AGILITY AND SPEED!

'WHAT THESE SIGNALS DO IS IMPOSE A *FITNESS COST* ON THE INDIVIDUAL THAT CANNOT BE BORNE BY THOSE WHO ARE NOT IN TOP CONDITION; THEY ARE *HONEST SIGNALS OF FITNESS*... PEACOCKS THAT ARE SICKLY OR WEAK, THEIR FEATHER DISPLAYS *SUCK.*'
– RATIONALSKEPTICISM.ORG

A SICK PEACOCK LOOKING DOWN IN THE DUMPS.

A HEALTHY PEACOCK SHOWING OFF!

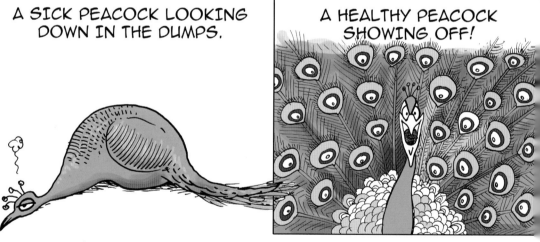

'DARWIN OBSERVED THAT THERE ARE SOME CHARACTERISTICS THAT DO NOT APPEAR TO HELP AN ORGANISM ADAPT TO ITS ENVIRONMENT AND ARE THUS NOT EXPLAINED BY *NATURAL SELECTION*. HE SUGGESTED THAT THEY FEATURE IN THE PROCESS OF *SEXUAL SELECTION.*'
– EMILY BROWN, CHRIST'S COLLEGE, CAMBRIDGE.

IN *THE DESCENT OF MAN AND SELECTION IN RELATION TO SEX* (1871) DARWIN SAID THAT SEXUAL SELECTION:

DEPENDS ON THE ADVANTAGE WHICH CERTAIN INDIVIDUALS HAVE OVER OTHER INDIVIDUALS OF THE SAME SEX AND SPECIES, IN EXCLUSIVE RELATION TO REPRODUCTION.

SO DARWIN NOTED THAT EVOLUTION IS DRIVEN BY NATURAL SELECTION AND SEXUAL SELECTION, OR AS THESE LADIES MAY PUT IT:

CUT THE CRAP AND SHOW US YOUR WILLY!

BUT SUCH EVOLUTION IS NOT SIMPLY A MATTER OF *CHANGE OVER TIME*, SINCE LOTS OF OTHER THINGS CHANGE OVER TIME. THE LEAVES ON TREES, FOR EXAMPLE, CHANGE OVER THE COURSE OF A YEAR.

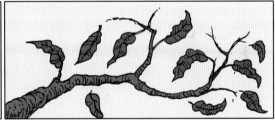

OR MOUNTAINS ERODE DOWN OVER THE COURSE OF A VERY LONG PERIOD OF TIME.

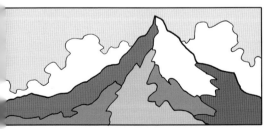

THESE ARE NOT *EVOLUTION* BECAUSE THEY DON'T INVOLVE DESCENT THROUGH *GENETIC INHERITANCE*.

THE CENTRAL IDEA OF **BIOLOGICAL EVOLUTION** IS THAT ALL LIFE ON EARTH SHARES A COMMON ANCESTOR... AND, THROUGH THE PROCESS OF **DESCENT** WITH **MODIFICATION**, IT LED TO THE DEVELOPMENT OF ALL THE DIVERSITY WE SEE NOW.

THIS IMAGE SHOWS THE **PHYLOGENY** – THE EVOLUTION OF A GENETICALLY RELATED GROUP, THE LINES OF DESCENT AND RELATIONSHIPS BETWEEN THEM.

OK, SO NOW LET'S LOOK MORE CLOSELY AT THE **CREATIONIST** VIEW. REMEMBER THAT SOME FORMS OF CREATIONISM SAY THAT THE TYPE OF NATURAL BIOLOGICAL PROCESSES WE HAVE JUST LOOKED AT **CANNOT** ACCOUNT FOR THE **HISTORY** AND **DIVERSITY** OF **LIFE ON EARTH:**

'*EVOLUTION* IS A *VALID PROCESS* (IN SCIENCE, BUSINESS, OR OTHERWISE); *CREATIONISTS* CERTAINLY AGREE WITH THIS – WHEN IT IS DIRECTED OR BUILT INTO THE DESIGN OF THINGS. CERTAINLY AUTOMOBILES HAVE IMPROVED DRAMATICALLY OVER THE PAST 100 YEARS, BUT IT *DIDN'T HAPPEN ALL BY ITSELF.* THE EVOLUTION OF THE AUTOMOBILE HAS BEEN DUE TO INTELLIGENT DESIGN INPUT, ADVANCED ENGINEERING SKILLS AND MANAGEMENT OVERSIGHT.' – *CREATIONISM.ORG*

HERE *CREATIONISTS* LIST SOME TYPES OF EVOLUTION, WITH NOT A LITTLE SARCASM. (NOTE THAT THEY ARE NOT AGAINST ALL TYPES OF EVOLUTION.)

#1 COSMIC:
From the theorized Big Bang of (estimated) 14-20 billion years ago to the (evolution or) generation of hydrogen gas into existence.

#2 CHEMICAL EVOLUTION:
Gases and other higher elements evolving into existence – increasing molecular & chemical order and complexity over time happening by itself.

#3 STAR & PLANETS:
Gravity, magnetism, radiation, and other 'accidentally existing' forces coalesce the molecules that evolved into existence all by themselves into proto-stars, then over billions of years into stars and planetary bodies.

#4 ORGANIC EVOLUTION:
Life emerging from sterile non-life by believed automatic advanced chemical processes. This has also been called spontaneous generation or more recently abiogenesis. Life from non-life; again, all by itself; increasing complexity and at some point in time – generating successive replication all by itself.

#5 MACRO-EVOLUTION:
Kinds of life diverging through random processes down through time. Single-celled creatures gave rise to multi-cellular marine organisms. Fish evolved into amphibians, and then into reptiles which evolved into the birds and mammals. Over the theorized millions of years the divergent complexity of life in nature has (apparently) increased in order, numbers and magnitude.

#6 MICRO-EVOLUTION:
Structured changes within pre-existing kinds of life. Heredity & variation. This one is scientific and is observable in nature.

SUMMARIZED FROM:
CREATIONISM.ORG

HERE ARE SOME INTERESTING POLL FINDINGS ABOUT AMERICANS' VIEWS REGARDING OUR ORIGINS:

Which of the following statements comes closest to your views on the origin and development of human beings?

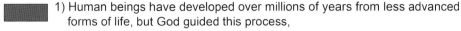 1) Human beings have developed over millions of years from less advanced forms of life, but God guided this process,

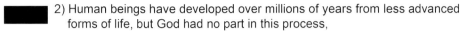 2) Human beings have developed over millions of years from less advanced forms of life, but God had no part in this process,

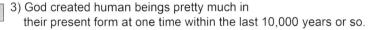 3) God created human beings pretty much in their present form at one time within the last 10,000 years or so.

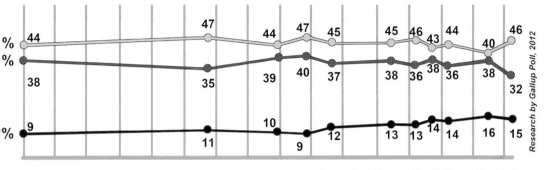

Research by Gallup Poll, 2012

Line 3 values: 44, 47, 44, 47, 45, 45, 46, 43, 44, 40, 46

Line 1 values: 38, 35, 39, 40, 37, 38, 36, 38, 36, 38, 32

Line 2 values: 9, 11, 10, 9, 12, 13, 13, 14, 14, 16, 15

Years: 1982 1984 1986 1988 1990 1992 1994 1996 1998 2000 2002 2004 2006 2008 2010 2012

WE CAN SEE FROM THIS THAT **46% OF AMERICANS** BELIEVE IN THE CREATIONIST VIEW '*THAT GOD CREATED HUMANS IN THEIR PRESENT FORM AT ONE TIME WITHIN THE LAST 10,000 YEARS*'.

THAT LEVEL IS PRETTY MUCH UNCHANGED FROM 30 YEARS AGO, WHEN GALLUP FIRST ASKED IT. THIS POSSIBLY MEANS THAT **SCIENTIFIC EDUCATION** IS NOT MAKING MUCH **PROGRESS** IN CHANGING **RELIGIOUS THINKING** IN THE US.

ALTHOUGH, THE AMOUNT OF PEOPLE WHO THINK **GOD** WAS **NOT INVOLVED** IN THE PROCESS OF HUMAN DEVELOPMENT HAS **INCREASED**.

THE IDEA **'THAT GOD CREATED HUMANS WITHIN THE LAST 10,000 YEARS'** IS THE POSITION OF YOUNG EARTH CREATIONISM. SOME OF THEM THINK IT WAS EVEN LESS, MAYBE ONLY **5,700 YEARS AGO.**

MIND YOU, IT'S NOT JUST **HUMANS** HE CREATED, BUT THE **UNIVERSE**, THE **EARTH** AND **ALL LIFE ON IT**. ALL IN SIX 24-HOUR DAYS...

SO, IT MEANS THAT THE YOUNG EARTH CREATIONIST FOLK BELIEVE THIS:

'WE BELIEVE THAT MAN WAS CREATED DIRECTLY BY GOD AND IN HIS IMAGE. WE BELIEVE THAT GOD CREATED THE HEAVENS AND THE EARTH, INCLUDING ALL LIFE, BY DIRECT ACT IN SIX LITERAL 24-HOUR DAYS ABOUT 6,000 YEARS AGO (GEN 1:1; JOHN 1:3; COL 1:16–17).

'THE... ACCOUNT OF ORIGINS AS PRESENTED IN GENESIS PROVIDES A RELIABLE FRAMEWORK FOR SCIENTIFIC RESEARCH INTO THE QUESTION OF THE ORIGIN AND HISTORY OF LIFE, MANKIND, THE EARTH AND THE UNIVERSE.

'THE VARIOUS ORIGINAL LIFE FORMS, INCLUDING MANKIND, WERE MADE BY DIRECT CREATIVE ACTS OF GOD. THE LIVING DESCENDANTS OF ANY OF THE ORIGINAL KINDS (APART FROM MAN) MAY REPRESENT MORE THAN ONE SPECIES TODAY, REFLECTING THE GENETIC POTENTIAL WITH THE ORIGINAL KIND. ONLY LIMITED BIOLOGICAL CHANGES HAVE OCCURRED NATURALLY WITHIN EACH KIND SINCE CREATION.'

PHEW!

CREATIONTODAY.ORG

QUITE A FEW CLAIMS THERE, AND THEY PRESENT SOME 'EVIDENCE' FOR THEM. HERE THEY ARE BELOW, ONE BY ONE.

AND WE HAVE AN INTERESTING GUY TO OFFER A REFUTATION OF THEM, *RICHY THOMPSON* OF THE *BRITISH HUMANIST ASSOCIATION.*

EVIDENCE FOR A YOUNG EARTH

THE OLDEST TREE. A BRISTLE CONE PINE IS APPROXIMATELY 4,300 YEARS OLD — DATED VIA TREE RINGS. THE METHOD MAY NOT BE PERFECT, BUT IT IS THE BEST WE HAVE FOR DATING TREES.

HELLO FOLKS!

THE OLDEST TREE IS IN FACT ESTIMATED TO BE **5,000** YEARS OLD, BUT THERE ARE CLONAL COLONIES THAT ARE **MUCH** OLDER THAN **CREATIONISTS' SUPPOSED** AGE OF THE EARTH, AND INDIVIDUAL MICRO-ORGANISMS THAT ARE OLDER TOO.

PANDO IS A CLONAL COLONY* OF **QUAKING ASPEN,** NEAR FICH LAKE IN UTAH. IT'S CONSIDERED TO COLLECTIVELY WEIGH **SIX MILLION KILOGRAMS** AND BE APPROXIMATELY **80,000 YEARS OLD!**

*A **CLONAL COLONY** OR **GENET** IS A GROUP OF GENETICALLY IDENTICAL INDIVIDUALS, LIKE PLANTS, FUNGI, ETC THAT HAVE GROWN IN ONE LOCATION, ALL ORIGINATING VEGETATIVELY (NOT SEXUALLY), FROM A SINGLE ANCESTOR. IN SOME CASES THEIR CONNECTED LINE GOES BACK WAY LONGER THAN 5,000 YEARS.

BUT THE OBVIOUS QUESTION IS: WHY DOES THINKING THE EARTH IS MILLIONS OF YEARS OLD MEAN THAT WE SHOULD EXPECT THAT THERE ARE TREES OR REEFS OLDER THAN A FEW THOUSAND YEARS?

I'M ALREADY IMPRESSED THAT **ANYTHING** HAS LASTED THAT LONG!

2ND CREATIONIST CLAIM: EARTH'S SLOWING ROTATION

'CALCULATIONS BASED UPON THE RATE OF THE SAHARA'S EXPANSION SHOW THE DESERT TO BE **4,000 YEARS OLD**. THIS YOUNG AGE OF THE SAHARA DESERT FITS QUITE WELL IN THE CREATIONIST TIME LINE, BEGINNING ITS DESERTIFICATION PROCESS SOON AFTER THE GLOBAL FLOOD. 'FOLLOWING THE EVOLUTIONIST TIME LINE OVER A PERIOD OF MILLIONS OF YEARS, THE SAHARA DESERT SHOULD HAVE **ALREADY** EXPANDED TO ITS **MAXIMUM SIZE**.'

Sahara Desert

AFRICA

IT'S RIDICULOUS TO ASSUME THAT THE SAHARA HAS ALWAYS EXISTED IN ITS CURRENT FORM. THE **WHOLE LAYOUT** OF THE CONTINENTS HAS CHANGED **REPEATEDLY**, FOR STARTERS!

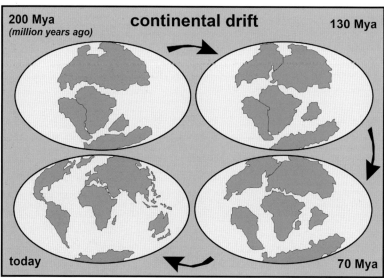

200 Mya (million years ago) — **continental drift** — 130 Mya

today — 70 Mya

AND THE CLIMATE OF EARTH OBVIOUSLY HASN'T STAYED CONSTANT OVER TIME – FOR EXAMPLE, THE LAST ICE AGE FINISHED **12,000 YEARS AGO**.

3RD CREATIONIST CLAIM: POPULATION

'IN 1810, ABOUT **ONE BILLION** PEOPLE LIVED ON EARTH. IN LESS THAN 200 YEARS, THE POPULATION HIT **SIX BILLION.** THIS FITS THE BIBLICAL CHRONOLOGY PERFECTLY AS THE CURRENT POPULATION STARTED ABOUT 4,400 YEARS AGO WITH **NOAH** AND HIS FAMILY AFTER THE FLOOD.'

IT SEEMS **CORRECT** THAT FOR MUCH OF HUMAN HISTORY POPULATION WAS FAIRLY CONSTANT...

BUT IT IS **RECENT TECHNOLOGICAL CHANGE** THAT HAS ALLOWED THE POPULATION TO EXPAND.

4TH CREATIONIST CLAIM: FAST-ERODING NIAGARA FALLS

'AFTER **CHARLES LYELL** PUBLISHED HIS **PRINCIPLES OF GEOLOGY**, SOCIETY BEGAN ACCEPTING THE THEORY THAT THE EARTH AND MANKIND EVOLVED... LYELL USED **NIAGARA FALLS** AS ONE OF HIS ILLUSTRATIONS TO PROMOTE **UNIFORMITARIANISM**. HE ESTIMATED THAT NIAGARA FALLS WAS 10,000 YEARS OLD. HE DID THIS TO TRY TO DISCREDIT THE BIBLE. SKEPTICS...LEAVE OUT ONE IMPORTANT FACTOR – A **WORLDWIDE FLOOD,** APPROXIMATELY 4,400 YEARS AGO...

'USING THE EVOLUTIONIST TIME FRAME, **NIAGARA FALLS** SHOULD HAVE **ALREADY** ERODED BACK INTO LAKE ERIE. THE REASON WHY NIAGARA FALLS HAS **NOT** ERODED FARTHER... CONTINUES TO ELUDE EVOLUTIONISTS. **SCIENCE** ALWAYS SEEMS TO CORRESPOND WITH THE **CREATION** TIMELINE WHILE **EVOLUTIONISTS** STRUGGLE TO MAKE THEIR ASSUMPTIONS AND THEORIES PLAUSIBLE.'

EXCEPT, THERE WAS **NO** WORLDWIDE FLOOD! RESEARCH IN VARIOUS FIELDS, SUCH AS TREE RINGS, POLAR CAPS, MOUNTAIN RANGES, FOSSIL RECORDS, GEOLOGICAL STRATA, ETC, HAS COME UP WITH **MANY** AND **VARIED** INDICATIONS THAT **NO SUCH WORLDWIDE FLOOD OCCURRED.**

JUST ONE SIMPLE EXAMPLE: TREE RING RECORDS GO BACK MORE THAN 10,000 YEARS, AND WE SEE **NO EVIDENCE** IN THEM OF A SUCH A WORLDWIDE EVENT AT THAT TIME.

SEE: NIN.TL/1KNLD1D

5TH CREATIONIST CLAIM: DECLINING MAGNETIC FIELD

'STUDIES OVER THE PAST 140 YEARS SHOW A CONSISTENT DECAY RATE IN THE EARTH'S MAGNETIC FIELD. AT THIS RATE, IN AS FEW AS 25,000 YEARS AGO, THE EARTH WOULD HAVE BEEN UNABLE TO SUPPORT LIFE BECAUSE OF THE HEAT FROM THE ELECTRIC CURRENT.'

SOME RESEARCH SUGGESTS THAT THE THEORIES OF **THOMAS G BARNES** ON THE MAGNETIC FIELDS WERE BASED ON DUBIOUS CALCULATIONS.

BARNES' STUDY RELIED ON OBSOLETE MODELS OF THE EARTH'S INTERIOR AND HE DID NOT MEASURE THE **TOTAL MAGNETIC FIELD** STRENGTH, ONLY THE **DIPOLE COMPONENT.**

6TH CREATIONIST CLAIM: SALT IN THE OCEANS

'THE WATER IN THE OCEANS CONTAINS 3.6% DISSOLVED MINERALS, GIVING THE OCEAN ITS **SALINITY**. SALT, COMPOSED OF THE ELEMENTS SODIUM AND CHLORINE, IS THE **PRIMARY MINERAL**. FOR YEARS, SCIENTISTS HAVE BEEN MEASURING THE AMOUNT OF SODIUM IN THE OCEANS AND HAVE FOUND THAT AN ESTIMATED **457 MILLION TONS** ARE DEPOSITED INTO THE OCEANS ANNUALLY, WHILE ONLY **122 MILLION TONS** LEAVE THE OCEAN VIA NUMEROUS METHODS. 'GIVEN THE CURRENT AMOUNT OF SALT IN THE OCEANS, THE DATA STRONGLY FAVORS A **RECENT CREATION** AND **GLOBAL FLOOD.** IF APPLIED TO THE EVOLUTIONIST'S TIME FRAME OF MILLIONS OF YEARS, THE OCEANS WOULD BE **SATURATED BY SALT.'**

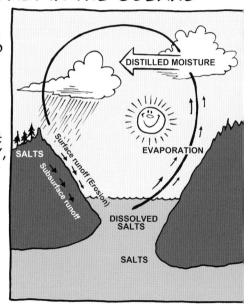

DISTILLED MOISTURE

Surface runoff (Erosion)

SALTS

Subsurface runoff

EVAPORATION

DISSOLVED SALTS

SALTS

AGAIN, THIS IS A CASE OF MISCALCULATIONS... THE **YOUNG EARTH** AUTHORS OMIT SOME MECHANISMS THAT REMOVE SODIUM FROM THE OCEANS.

AND A MORE DETAILED ANALYSIS SHOWS THAT THE AMOUNT OF SODIUM **ADDED** ROUGHLY MATCHES THE AMOUNT **REMOVED.**

THIS **'OLD EARTH'** CREATIONIST WEBSITE REFUTES VARIOUS OF THE **'YOUNG EARTH'** CLAIMS:
NIN.TL/REFUTINGYOUNGEARTH

THE TYPE OF THINKING ABOVE FROM THE YOUNG EARTH CREATIONISTS, WHERE ANYTHING IS MADE TO 'FIT' THEIR THEORY, WILL BE LOOKED AT MORE CLOSELY LATER. BUT JUST FOR A QUICK LOOK NOW...

HERE WE HAVE **DAVE** WHO THINKS THAT **DOGS** ARE **SPIES FROM VENUS** WHO ARE PREPARING FOR **DOG SPACESHIPS** TO COME AND **INVADE EARTH**. A MAD IDEA, BUT IS IT ANY MORE OUTRAGEOUS THAN WHAT IS TAKEN AS **COMMONPLACE** IN SOME RELIGIONS?

HOW ABOUT BELIEVING THAT **GOD** SPOKE TO YOU IN THE DESERT, TEACHING HOLY RULES... OR THAT A **CELESTIAL BEING** WILL **HATE** YOU UNLESS YOU EAT **FISH** ON A **FRIDAY**... OR SIGNING ON IN A CHURCH FOR A SPECIFIED **BILLION YEARS**?

DAVE'S FRIENDS TRY TO PRESENT LOGICAL, REASONED ARGUMENTS TO SHOW THE **INCONSISTENCY** OF HIS IDEAS. BUT DAVE ALWAYS COMES UP WITH **INGENIOUS** WAYS TO SAVE HIS CENTRAL THEORY, EVEN IF THE **EVIDENCE** SEEMS OVERWHELMINGLY AGAINST IT. HE WILL **TWIST AND TURN** TO MAKE SURE THE EVIDENCE **FITS**...

IT'S ONLY A MATTER OF **WEEKS**!

THE SPACESHIPS WILL ARRIVE AND THEN YOU'LL WISH YOU'D LISTENED TO ME! WE'VE GOTTA ACT **NOW** – LET THE GOVERNMENT KNOW!

LOOK, DAVE, DOGS ARE OBVIOUSLY **NOT** SPACE INVADERS. THEY'RE JUST **DUMB PETS**. THEY CAN'T EVEN **SPEAK** – HOW ARE THEY GONNA **COMMUNICATE** WITH **VENUS**?

THEY **CAN** SPEAK!

THEY JUST CHOOSE TO **HIDE** IT FROM US! THEY WAIT TILL WE LEAVE THE **ROOM**, THEN THEY'RE **CHATTING** AWAY TEN TO THE **DOZEN**!

BUT WHAT ABOUT *VENUS*? IT'S HORRENDOUSLY HOT, WITH GREAT SWATHES OF ACID CLOUDS. NOTHING COULD LIVE THERE. CERTAINLY NOT A *DOG*!

TCCK!

THEY DON'T LIVE ON THE *SURFACE*, PETE, YOU IDIOT - THEY LIVE *BELOW*, DOWN IN *UNDERGROUND BUNKERS*.

BUT HOW DO THE DOGS ON EARTH *COMMUNICATE* WITH THE DOGS ON VENUS?

I'VE GOT A DOG AND I'M PRETTY SURE HE'S NOT GOT A *TRANSMITTER* HIDDEN IN HIS BASKET!

LAUGH ALL YOU WANT, BUT YOU'LL *REGRET* IT ONE DAY.

HAHA HA!

ANYWAY, THE *TRANSMITTERS* ARE IN THEIR *BRAINS!*

DOG

YOU CAN SEE HOW THIS MIGHT GO ON *AD NAUSEAM*. MARY AND PETE KEEP COMING UP WITH WHAT SEEM LIKE CLEAR POINTS CONTRADICTING DAVE'S THEORY, BUT DAVE ALWAYS COMES BACK WITH SOME *NEW TWIST* THAT ALLOWS HIS THEORY TO FIT THE EVIDENCE. THIS OFTEN SEEMS TO BE WHAT *CREATIONISTS* DO – NO MATTER *WHAT* SCIENTIFIC EVIDENCE IS DEVELOPED, THEY REACT WITH A NEW TWIST THAT ALLOWS THEIR CENTRAL BELIEF TO REMAIN *UNTARNISHED*.

TAKE A KEY ELEMENT IN THE YOUNG EARTH CREATIONIST IDEA – *THE FLOOD.* NOAH BUILT HIS ARK AND TOOK IN 'TWO OF ALL LIVING CREATURES, BOTH MALE AND FEMALE, AND SEVEN PAIRS OF ALL THE CLEAN ANIMALS'.

HMMM... MUST HAVE BEEN *PRETTY CROWDED* ON AN ARK SAID TO HAVE MEASURED 460 X 74 X 44 FEET. HOW DID THEY *GET IN* ALL THOSE ANIMALS?

HOW ABOUT THE BIG DINOSAURS? THE BRONTOSAURUS *ALONE* WAS *75 FEET LONG!*

AND HOW DID FAR-AWAY ANIMALS LIKE THE *POLAR BEARS* GET ALL THE WAY TO *MOUNT ARARAT* IN TURKEY?

I THOUGHT I TOLD YOU TO STAY OFF THE SALAD DRESSING!

WELL, I HAVE PUT ON A LITTLE WEIGHT...

PACK YOUR SHORTS, DEAR, IT'S WARM DOWN THERE.

AND HOW DID NOAH *FEED* ALL THOSE ANIMALS DURING THE YEAR OF THE FLOOD? THAT'S A *LOT* OF PACKED LUNCHES!

WE ARE FOCUSING HERE MOSTLY ON **YOUNG EARTH CREATIONISM**, BUT THERE ARE OTHER TYPES. FOR EXAMPLE:

THE **'OLD EARTH'** TYPE ACCEPTS THAT THE EARTH IS **FAR OLDER** THAN 6,000 YEARS, BUT STILL DOES NOT ACCEPT **EVOLUTION**. WHILE THIS INVOLVES REJECTING A LITERAL INTERPRETATION OF THE BIBLE, IT DOES NOT QUITE ACCEPT SEEING THE **GENESIS** STORY AS PURELY METAPHORICAL, AS THE **THEISTIC EVOLUTIONIST** VIEW HAS IT.

AH, THAT WAS ABOUT 90 MILLION YEARS AGO. THOSE DINOS REALLY KNEW HOW TO PARTY!

THEISTIC EVOLUTIONISTS THINK THAT **SCIENCE** AND **RELIGIOUS BELIEFS** CAN BE COMPATIBLE. THEY SUGGEST THAT GOD CREATED THE WORLD BY SETTING THE **COSMIC** AND **BIOLOGICAL** PROCESSES IN **MOTION**...

BUT THEN **WITHDREW**, AND LET **EVOLUTION** TAKE ITS COURSE.

THE **CREATION SCIENCE** VIEW, MEANWHILE, INVOLVES A LITERAL ACCEPTANCE OF THE BIBLE, AND CREATION WITHIN THE LAST 6,000 YEARS. IT THEREFORE **REJECTS** EVOLUTION, BUT ATTEMPTS TO PROVIDE *"SCIENTIFIC SUPPORT"* FOR THE **GENESIS** CREATION STORY.

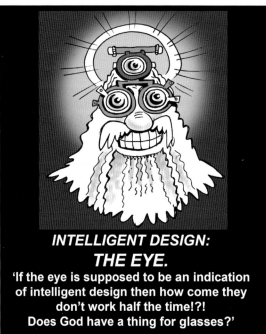

INTELLIGENT DESIGN: THE EYE.

'If the eye is supposed to be an indication of intelligent design then how come they don't work half the time!?! Does God have a thing for glasses?'

INTELLIGENT DESIGN IS A RECENT TYPE OF CREATIONISM, AND ALSO PSEUDOSCIENTIFIC. IT SUGGESTS THAT THE **INTRICATE DESIGN** OF THE UNIVERSE IS BEST EXPLAINED BY SOME **DELIBERATE INTELLIGENT CAUSE,** THOUGH NOT ALL OF THEM CLAIM THIS TO BE THE WORK OF A CHRISTIAN GOD.

THESE VIEWS ARE ALL REJECTED BY HUMANISTS AS WELL AS BY MOST SCIENTISTS.

INDEED, **MOST TYPES** OF CREATIONISM ARE REJECTED BY MANY RELIGIOUS PEOPLE TOO, WHO ARE OFTEN EMBARRASSED BY CREATIONISTS' REFUSAL TO ACCEPT THE BASIC PRINCIPLES OF SCIENCE AND EVOLUTION.

A KEY ISSUE THAT HAS CAUSED A LOT OF BITTER DISAGREEMENT IS **SHOULD CREATIONISM BE TAUGHT IN SCHOOLS?** SHOULD PUBLIC FUNDS BE USED IN THE PROMOTION OF **EXTREME RELIGIOUS VIEWS** REGARDING THE NATURE OF **LIFE** AND THE **UNIVERSE?**

HERE'S ANOTHER INTERESTING GUY TO HELP US OUT: **STEPHEN LAW** IS A SENIOR LECTURER IN PHILOSOPHY (UNIVERSITY OF LONDON), EDITOR OF THE ROYAL INSTITUTE OF PHILOSOPHY JOURNAL 'THINK', AND PROVOST OF 'CENTRE FOR INQUIRY UK'.

YOUNG EARTH CREATIONISM CONTINUES TO BE TAUGHT IN SCHOOLS IN THE UK AND THE US.

OFTEN, THIS TEACHING IS DONE COVERTLY.

I KNOW OF TWO LEADING INDEPENDENT BRITISH SCHOOLS WHERE IT HAS BEEN TAUGHT BY A SCIENCE TEACHER WITHOUT THE KNOWLEDGE OR PERMISSION OF THE SCHOOL.

OBVIOUSLY I OBJECT TO YOUNG EARTH CREATIONISM BEING TAUGHT AS A RIVAL TO ORTHODOX SCIENTIFIC THEORIES.

PEOPLE OFTEN OBJECT TO THE TEACHING OF IT ON THE GROUNDS THAT CHILDREN SHOULD NOT BE TAUGHT THINGS KNOWN TO BE FALSE.

BUT THAT IS NOT MY MAIN OBJECTION (THOUGH TEACHING KNOWN FALSEHOODS IS BAD ENOUGH). MY MAIN OBJECTION IS THIS: TEACHING CHILDREN THAT YOUNG EARTH CREATIONISM IS SCIENTIFICALLY RESPECTABLE INVOLVES TEACHING CHILDREN TO THINK LIKE **DAVE** FROM A FEW PAGES BACK!

STEPHENLAW.BLOGSPOT.JP

THE BRITISH HUMANIST ASSOCIATION (BHA) AND THE AMERICAN HUMANIST ASSOCATION (AHA), AND MANY OTHER GROUPS, THINK THAT EVOLUTION IS THE MOST IMPORTANT IDEA UNDERLYING BIOLOGICAL SCIENCE. IT IS A **KEY CONCEPT** THAT CHILDREN SHOULD BE INTRODUCED TO AT AN EARLY STAGE SO AS TO PROTECT THEM FROM POPULAR MISCONCEPTIONS.

AND IT HELPS ENSURE A FIRM SCIENTIFIC UNDERSTANDING WHEN THEY STUDY IT IN MORE DEPTH LATER ON.

SPECIFICALLY WITH REGARD TO BIOLOGY CLASSES: AN UNDERSTANDING OF EVOLUTION IS **CENTRAL** TO UNDERSTANDING **ALL ASPECTS OF BIOLOGY,** FROM HUMAN BEHAVIOR TO THE GENETIC BASIS OF DISEASE.

IT IS ALSO **KEY** TO UNDERSTANDING HOW THE ENVIRONMENT AFFECTS THE **DEVELOPMENT** AND **DIVERSITY** OF LIFE ON EARTH.

AS SUCH, IT SHOULD BE A **CENTRAL FEATURE** OF, NOT **MARGINAL TO**, SCHOOL BIOLOGY.

BEFORE WE LOOK AT THE SCHOOLS SITUATION IN THE *US* AND THE *UK* LET'S CONSIDER A BIT MORE ABOUT WHY CREATIONISM SHOULD *NOT* BE TAUGHT IN SCHOOLS.

ONE OF THE *KEY THINGS* PEOPLE SAY TO THIS IS THAT SUCH RELIGIOUS THINKING DOES NOT FOSTER THE KIND OF INQUIRING MINDS THAT GO OUT AND MAKE *NEW DISCOVERIES* OR THAT COME UP WITH *SCIENTIFIC BREAKTHROUGHS.*

RICHARD DAWKINS HAS SOUND ADVICE FOR US HERE:

CHRISTOPHER HITCHENS STATES IT EVEN MORE FORCEFULLY, AS WAS HIS WONT.

DO NOT *INDOCTRINATE* YOUR CHILDREN. TEACH THEM HOW TO *THINK FOR THEMSELVES,* HOW TO *EVALUATE EVIDENCE,* AND HOW TO *DISAGREE WITH YOU.*

CONTAMINATING A CHILD'S MIND BEFORE IT HAS DEVELOPED CRITICAL THINKING SKILLS IS *NEARLY AS BAD* AS *SEXUALLY ABUSING THEIR BODIES.*

IF RELIGIOUS INSTRUCTION WERE NOT ALLOWED UNTIL THE *AGE OF REASON,* WE WOULD BE LIVING IN A *QUITE DIFFERENT WORLD!*

A FURTHER CONNECTED POINT IS WELL MADE BY *NOAM CHOMSKY,* WHO NOTED THAT PEOPLE THINKING IN SIMPLISTIC RELIGIOUS WAYS HAVE A LOT OF *POWER* AND DO A LOT OF *DAMAGE.*

STUPID PEOPLE HAVE *POWER...*AND THEY ARE CARRYING OUT ACTIONS THAT *DEFUND* EFFORTS TO DO SOMETHING ABOUT THE *SERIOUS ENVIRONMENTAL PROBLEMS* THAT FACE US.

FOR EXAMPLE, THE REPUBLICAN HEAD OF A CONGRESSIONAL SUB-COMMITTEE SAID THAT GLOBAL WARMING *CAN'T BE A PROBLEM* BECAUSE *GOD PROMISED NOAH* THAT THERE WOULDN'T BE *ANOTHER FLOOD.*

BRUCE BARTLETT, A DOMESTIC POLICY ADVISER TO RONALD REAGAN, ONCE GAVE US AN EXAMPLE OF SUCH STUPID PEOPLE IN POWER. IN THIS CASE **GEORGE W BUSH.**

'HE TRULY BELIEVES HE'S ON A MISSION FROM GOD. ABSOLUTE FAITH LIKE THAT OVERWHELMS A NEED FOR ANALYSIS. THE WHOLE THING ABOUT FAITH IS TO BELIEVE THINGS FOR WHICH THERE IS NO EMPIRICAL EVIDENCE... BUT, YOU CAN'T RUN THE WORLD ON FAITH.'

HOW WELL DID THINGS GO FOR THE UNITED STATES WHEN A **RELIGIOUS MAN** THOUGHT WITH HIS **GUT,** DOWNGRADING ANALYSIS OF **FACTS** AND AVOIDING **VIEWPOINTS** THAT **DID NOT ALREADY MATCH HIS?**

HMM... NOT SO WELL.

FAITH IS THE SURRENDER OF THE **MIND,** THE SURRENDER OF **REASON**... THE SURRENDER OF THE **ONLY THING** THAT MAKES US **DIFFERENT** FROM OTHER MAMMALS.

CHRISTOPHER HITCHENS AGAIN.

OUR NEED TO **BELIEVE,** TO SURRENDER OUR **SKEPTICISM** AND OUR **REASON,** OUR YEARNING TO DISCARD THAT... AND INSTEAD TO PUT ALL OUR TRUST OR FAITH IN **SOMEONE** OR **SOMETHING**...

TO ME, THAT IS A **SINISTER THING.**

AS FOR THE TEACHING OF **CREATIONISM** IN **US SCHOOLS**: IT'S BEEN A REAL BACK-AND-FORTH BATTLE – THERE'S BEEN A STRONG PUSH BY CONSERVATIVE RELIGIOUS GROUPS TO ENSURE THAT *'STUDENTS CRITICALLY ANALYZE KEY ASPECTS OF EVOLUTIONARY THEORY'.*

A KEY RULING BY THE SUPREME COURT AGAINST THIS CAME IN *1968*, WHEN, IN *EPPERSON V ARKANSAS*, IT INSISTED THAT ARKANSAS'S LAW PROHIBITING THE TEACHING OF *EVOLUTION* WAS A *VIOLATION OF THE FIRST AMENDMENT.*

HOWEVER, LOUISIANA THEN PASSED A LAW REQUIRING THAT PUBLIC SCHOOLS SHOULD GIVE *'EQUAL TIME TO ALTERNATIVE THEORIES OF ORIGIN'.*

AND LIKE A GAME OF CONSTITUTIONAL TENNIS, IN THE LATE 1980S THE SUPREME COURT RULED **UNCONSTITUTIONAL** THE PROCESS REQUIRING **CREATION** TO BE TAUGHT ALONGSIDE *EVOLUTION*.

RECENTLY, PROPONENTS OF 'INTELLIGENT DESIGN' HAVE BEEN PUSHING FOR THIS TO BE TAUGHT IN PUBLIC SCHOOLS IN THEIR *'TEACH THE CONTROVERSY'* CAMPAIGN – PRESENTING STUDENTS WITH EVIDENCE FOR AND AGAINST EVOLUTION.

IMAGE FROM AMORPHIA APPAREL'S 'TEACH THE CONTROVERSY' T-SHIRT RANGE.

OPPONENTS SAY IT SHOULD NOT BE TAUGHT BECAUSE IT IS *PSEUDOSCIENCE* – ITS CLAIMS CANNOT BE TESTED BY EXPERIMENT NOR DOES IT PROPOSE ANY NEW HYPOTHESES, AND ITS PREDICTIONS, WHEN IT *DOES* MAKE THEM, ARE WRONG.

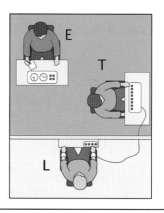

THERE IS *NO ACTUAL SCIENTIFIC CONTROVERSY*, ONLY A *POLITICAL* AND *RELIGIOUS* ONE. SO, SOME SAY THAT 'TEACHING THE CONTROVERSY' MIGHT BE *OK* IN A SOCIAL STUDIES OR PHILOSOPHY CLASS.

OTHERS REJECT *ALL* TEACHING OF CREATIONISM TO CHILDREN AS A MATTER OF PRINCIPLE. SOME GO SO FAR AS TO SAY THAT IT'S AKIN TO *CHILD ABUSE*, IN THE MENTAL DAMAGE IT CAN DO.

PHYSICS PROFESSOR LAWRENCE KRAUSS:

THAT IDEA THAT WE SHOULDN'T OFFEND RELIGIOUS BELIEFS BY REQUIRING KIDS TO KNOW, TO UNDERSTAND REALITY – THAT'S CHILD ABUSE...

TEACHING KIDS THE NOTION THAT THE EARTH IS 6,000 YEARS OLD IS LIKE TEACHING KIDS THAT THE DISTANCE ACROSS THE UNITED STATES IS 17 FEET. THAT'S HOW BIG AN ERROR IT IS.

THE PURPOSE OF EDUCATION IS NOT TO VALIDATE IGNORANCE, BUT TO OVERCOME IT.

OF COURSE, PARENTS WHO **WANT** TO SEND THEIR CHILDREN TO PRIVATE RELIGIOUS SCHOOLS ARE FREE TO DO SO. THE ISSUE IN THE **US** IS THAT TAXPAYERS' MONEY SHOULD NOT BE USED FOR RELIGIOUS INSTRUCTION, ESPECIALLY IN A SYSTEM ALREADY SHORT OF CASH. THIS MAP SHOWS THE LOCATION OF SCHOOLS RECEIVING PUBLIC FUNDING THAT TEACH CREATIONISM:

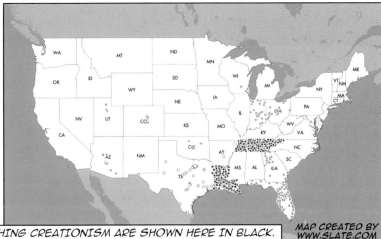

MAP CREATED BY WWW.SLATE.COM

PUBLIC SCHOOLS TEACHING CREATIONISM ARE SHOWN HERE IN BLACK. CHARTER SCHOOLS TEACHING IT ARE SHOWN IN WHITE CIRCLES, AND PRIVATE SCHOOLS IN GREY.

TENNESSEE

YOU CAN SEE THAT SUCH SCHOOLS ARE MOSTLY IN THE SOUTHERN STATES OF THE US. FOR EXAMPLE, **FLORIDA** HAS AT LEAST 164 SCHOOLS THAT TEACH CREATIONISM. **TEXAS, LOUISIANA** AND **TENNESSEE** PERMIT PUBLIC SCHOOL TEACHERS TO TEACH 'ALTERNATIVES' TO EVOLUTION OR EVEN OPT OUT OF TEACHING IT.

IN SEVERAL STATES, TAXPAYER MONEY IS FUNDING CREATIONIST PRIVATE SCHOOLS VIA STATE TUITION VOUCHERS OR SCHOLARSHIP PROGRAMS. SOME PEOPLE IN THE **US** ARE UNHAPPY THAT THEIR TAX MONEY IS HELPING TO CONVINCE STUDENTS THAT **EVOLUTION** IS A SCIENTIFIC HYPOTHESIS NO MORE CREDIBLE THAN **'GOD DID IT'**. A COALITION OF GROUPS OPPOSE THIS, INCLUDING THE AMERICAN FEDERATION OF TEACHERS, THE AMERICAN CIVIL LIBERTIES UNION, THE NATIONAL PARENT TEACHER ASSOCIATION AND THE NATIONAL ORGANIZATION FOR WOMEN.

BUT NOT JUST THERE, AS PROFESSOR OF BIOLOGY **RANDY MOORE** (UNIVERSITY OF MINNESOTA), TOLD THE NEW YORK TIMES:

CREATIONISTS ARE IN THE CLASSROOM, AND IT'S NOT JUST THE SOUTH. AT LEAST **25%** OF HIGH-SCHOOL TEACHERS IN MINNESOTA EXPLICITLY TEACH CREATIONISM.

SCIENCE

THE NY TIMES ARTICLE NOTED THAT ONLY **28%** OF BIOLOGY TEACHERS CONSISTENTLY FOLLOW THE RECOMMENDATIONS OF THE **US NATIONAL RESEARCH COUNCIL** TO DESCRIBE EVIDENCE FOR EVOLUTION AND EXPLAIN HOW IT IS AN IMPORTANT UNIFYING THEME IN ALL OF BIOLOGY. AND THAT **13%** ADVOCATE CREATIONISM, SPENDING AT LEAST AN HOUR OF CLASS TIME PRESENTING IT IN A POSITIVE LIGHT.

THEN WE HAVE WHAT ARE CALLED '**THE CAUTIOUS 60%.**' – THOSE TEACHERS WHO AVOID TROUBLE FROM PARENTS, STUDENTS AND PERHAPS FELLOW TEACHERS BY ENDORSING NEITHER *EVOLUTION* NOR *CREATIONISM.* DOESN'T THAT SOUND LIKE *FEAR* DEFEATING *SCIENCE? CONFORMISM* DEFEATING *FREE ENQUIRY?*

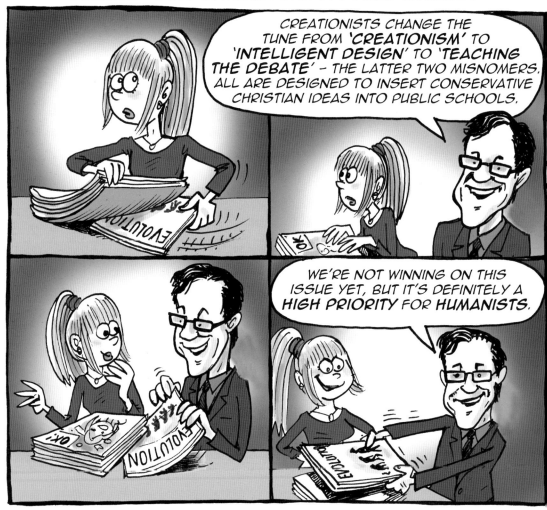

ROY SPECKHARDT, EXECUTIVE DIRECTOR OF THE AMERICAN HUMANIST ASSOCIATION.

WITH IMPORTANT ISSUES AT STAKE, IT'S NOT SURPRISING THAT HUMANISTS IN THE UK AND THE US HAVE MADE SUCH A BIG EFFORT TO PROMOTE SCIENCE IN EDUCATION AND TO DISCOURAGE WASTING TIME AND MONEY ON TEACHING CREATIONISM.

AS FOR THE UK:

THE **BHA** CO-ORDINATED THE 'TEACH EVOLUTION, NOT CREATIONISM' CAMPAIGN, WHICH WAS ALSO SUPPORTED BY ORGANIZATIONS SUCH AS THE **ASSOCIATION FOR SCIENCE EDUCATION** AND THE **BRITISH SCIENCE ASSOCIATION.**

AND BY SCIENTISTS LIKE SIR DAVID ATTENBOROUGH, PROFESSOR COLIN BLAKEMORE, PROFESSOR RICHARD DAWKINS, SIR PAUL NURSE AND REVD PROFESSOR MICHAEL REISS.

TO SUMMARIZE OUR POSITION: WE THINK THERE'S MORE THE [BRITISH] GOVERNMENT CAN DO TO STOP CREATIONISM BEING TAUGHT IN STATE SCHOOLS, PARTICULARLY IN MAINTAINED SCHOOLS, WHERE THE EXISTING GUIDANCE ON THE MATTER HAS BEEN WITHDRAWN.

WE ALSO HAVE CONCERNS ABOUT THE SCRUTINY OF PROPOSALS FOR 'FREE SCHOOLS', PARTICULARLY IN THE FIRST FEW YEARS OF THE PROGRAM, WHERE THERE ARE A NUMBER OF PROBLEM CASES.

THE BHA HAS PRODUCED A PACK ON HOW THESE ISSUES RELATE TO EDUCATION. YOU CAN SEE SOME MORE AT THE BACK OF THE BOOK.

RICHY WILL WALK US THROUGH THE SITUATION IN THE UK:

WITH INDEPENDENT SCHOOLS THE BIG ISSUE IS THE LACK OF CONCERN SHOWN BY **OFSTED*** WITH RESPECT TO THE TEACHING OF PSEUDOSCIENCE – SUCH TEACHING SHOULD, AT THE VERY LEAST, CAUSE A SCHOOL TO BE MARKED DOWN SIGNIFICANTLY, BUT CURRENTLY IT DOESN'T.

ALTHOUGH THE RECENT ADDITION OF EVOLUTION TO THE PRIMARY CURRICULUM IS HUGELY SIGNIFICANT.

*THE OFFICE FOR STANDARDS IN EDUCATION, CHILDREN'S SERVICES AND SKILLS.

OBVIOUSLY WE WANT THE TEACHING OF CREATIONISM AS SCIENTIFICALLY VALID TO BE PRECLUDED AND FOR EVOLUTION TO BE A REQUIREMENT TO BE TAUGHT. ALTHOUGH THAT IS NOT TO SAY THAT **CREATIONISM** CANNOT BE TAUGHT IN RELIGIOUS EDUCATION CLASSES, AS SOMETHING THAT MANY PEOPLE BELIEVE IN.

BUT PREFERABLY EVEN **THAT** SHOULDN'T HAPPEN AT TOO YOUNG AN AGE, WHEN CHILDREN CAN'T UNDERSTAND THE DIFFERENCE BETWEEN BEING TAUGHT **FACT** AND BEING TAUGHT ABOUT AN **OPINION** – SOMETHING THAT IS A FREQUENT PROBLEM WITH PRIMARY SCHOOLS IN PARTICULAR.

FREE SCHOOLS NOW HAVE RULES IN PLACE IN THEIR FUNDING AGREEMENTS REQUIRING THEM TO TEACH **EVOLUTION** AND PRECLUDING THE TEACHING OF **PSEUDOSCIENCE** IN THE CURRICULUM. THIS ISN'T PERFECT, AS THE **DEPARTMENT FOR EDUCATION** TELLS US THAT IT **DOESN'T** COVER **COLLECTIVE WORSHIP** – PERHAPS WHERE THE ISSUE IS MOST LIKELY TO ARISE!

GOVERNMENT ADVICE ON TEACHING SCIENCE

MAINTAINED SCHOOLS MUST TEACH THE NATIONAL CURRICULUM, INCLUDING A MODULE ON EVOLUTION FROM YEAR SIX. SOON ALSO FOR A-LEVEL EXAMS... HOWEVER THERE'S NOTHING PRECLUDING THE TEACHING OF **PSEUDOSCIENCE**, JUST GENERAL GOVERNMENT STATEMENTS THAT THIS SHOULD NOT HAPPEN.

OBVIOUSLY WE THINK THAT **NO CHILD** SHOULD BE TAUGHT **CREATIONISM** AS SCIENTIFICALLY VALID, WHETHER IN A **STATE** OR A **PRIVATE** SCHOOL. HOWEVER, I THINK IT'S COMPLICATED, FROM A HUMAN RIGHTS PERSPECTIVE, AS TO WHETHER OR NOT IT COULD BE BANNED.

A **LEGAL POSITIVE STEP** WOULD BE FOR INDEPENDENT SCHOOLS TO START BEING INSPECTED ON IT **PROPERLY** BY OFSTED, AND NOT SIMPLY GIVEN A FREE PASS.

IN THE UK THERE ARE THREE MAIN NETWORKS OF PRIVATE SCHOOLS WHERE CREATIONISM, OF ONE TYPE OF ANOTHER, IS TAUGHT:

> ☆ **ACCELERATED CHRISTIAN EDUCATION NETWORK,** (A PARTICULARLY CRAZY AMERICAN IMPORT)
> ☆ **CHRISTIAN SCHOOLS' TRUST NETWORK.**
> ☆ **EXCLUSIVE BRETHREN SCHOOLS, OFTEN CALLED THE FOCUS LEARNING TRUST.**

ON TOP OF THAT, MANY (MOST?) MUSLIM AND JEWISH PRIVATE SCHOOLS WILL BE **CREATIONIST**. AND WE HAVE CONCERNS ABOUT THE STEINER SCHOOLS TOO.

SINCE 2008, GROUPS OF PRIVATE SCHOOLS HAVE BEEN ABLE TO CHOOSE TO SET UP THEIR OWN INSPECTORATES, OF WHICH **OFSTED** HAS OVERSIGHT. THIS IS SUPPOSEDLY SO THE INSPECTORS CAN BE MORE SENSITIVE TO THE SCHOOLS' PARTICULAR NEEDS, ALTHOUGH IN PRACTICE IT MEANS TURNING **EVEN MORE** OF A BLIND EYE TO PSEUDOSCIENCE.

THE UK HAS ONE **CREATIONIST ZOO** CALLED **NOAH'S ARK ZOO FARM.** RECENTLY IT WAS AWARDED **LEARNING OUTSIDE THE CLASSROOM'S** QUALITY BADGE. AS THIS IS **GOVERNMENT-ENDORSED,** WE WROTE TO THEN SECRETARY OF STATE FOR EDUCATION, **MICHAEL GOVE,** TO ASK HIM TO CHALLENGE THIS AWARD.

WE'VE YET TO HEAR BACK ON THAT...

CLASS IV
THE SCIENCE OF GOD'S LOVE

THE **CHRISTIAN SCHOOLS' TRUST** AND ALL PRIVATE **MUSLIM** SCHOOLS ARE BOTH INSPECTED BY THE **BRIDGE SCHOOLS INSPECTORATE,** WHEREAS THE **EXCLUSIVE BRETHREN** AND **STEINER SCHOOLS** ARE INSPECTED BY THE **SCHOOL INSPECTION SERVICE.**

STOP PRESS!: IN JUNE 2014, WHILE WE WERE MAKING THIS BOOK, THE UK GOVERNMENT BANNED ALL ENGLISH STATE SCHOOLS FROM TEACHING PSEUDOSCIENTIFIC IDEAS SUCH AS CREATIONISM AS SCIENTIFICALLY VALID – SO WE'RE ALL MAKING GOOD PROGRESS.

OF COURSE SOME RELIGIOUS PEOPLE MAKE THE POINT THAT PLENTY OF SCIENTISTS ARE RELIGIOUS AND THAT THERE NEED NOT BE A CONTRADICTION INVOLVED.

A STUDY AT RICE UNIVERSITY'S RELIGION AND PUBLIC LIFE PROGRAM, BASED ON A SURVEY OF 10,000 US ADULTS, FOUND THAT:

- NEARLY 36% OF SCIENTISTS HAVE NO DOUBT ABOUT GOD'S EXISTENCE
- 18% OF SCIENTISTS ATTENDED WEEKLY RELIGIOUS SERVICES (COMPARED WITH 20% OF THE GENERAL US POPULATION)
- 15% OF SCIENTISTS CONSIDER THEMSELVES VERY RELIGIOUS (COMPARED WITH 19% GENERALLY)

THOUGH THESE FIGURES LOOK LOW COMPARED TO THE FAR HIGHER % WHO BELIEVE IN GOD AMONG THE GENERAL US POPULATION.

WE CAN RESPOND TO THIS BY SAYING: **YES,** SIMPLY **BEING RELIGIOUS** DOESN'T NECESSARILY MEAN HOLDING BELIEFS THAT ACTIVELY GO AGAINST **SCIENTIFIC EVIDENCE** AND **CONSENSUS.**

BUT IT **DOES** MEAN HOLDING BELIEFS THAT ARE UNSUPPORTED BY THE EVIDENCE (THE SO-CALLED 'LEAP OF FAITH'). AND MOST (THOUGH BY NO MEANS ALL) INDIVIDUALS FIND THIS TENDS NOT TO FIT IN WITH HAVING A SCIENTIFIC WORLDVIEW.

MY FAITH WILL CARRY ME OVER THE WATER!

GENERALLY, A SCIENTIFIC MINDSET MEANS **BEING SKEPTICAL** OF CLAIMS, DEMANDING GOOD EVIDENCE AND **REJECTING** CLAIMS FOR WHICH EVIDENCE IS NOT FORTHCOMING.

BEING A CREATIONIST, OR BELIEVING IN HOMEOPATHY, AND SO ON, MEANS **FALLING DOWN** ON THOSE FRONTS.

SPLASH!

HERE'S A RATHER TONGUE-IN-CHEEK PROJECT, WITH A SERIOUS POINT UNDERLYING IT: *PROJECT STEVE*

PROJECT STEVE IS A LIST OF SCIENTISTS NAMED STEVEN OR SIMILAR (STEPHANIE, STEFAN, ESTEBAN, ETC) WHO 'SUPPORT EVOLUTION'. IT WAS CREATED BY THE *NATIONAL CENTER FOR SCIENCE EDUCATION* AS A PARODY OF LISTS OF SCIENTISTS WHO 'DOUBT EVOLUTION', SUCH AS THE *DISCOVERY INSTITUTE'S* ...

A SCIENTIFIC DISSENT FROM DARWINISM

"We are skeptical of claims for the ability of random mutation and natural selection to account for the complexity of life. Careful examination of the evidence for Darwinian theory should be encouraged."

THE *PROJECT STEVE* LIST POKES FUN AT SUCH ENDEAVORS, TO MAKE IT CLEAR THAT:

WE DID NOT WISH TO MISLEAD THE PUBLIC INTO THINKING THAT SCIENTIFIC ISSUES ARE DECIDED BY WHO HAS THE LONGER LIST OF SCIENTISTS!

INSTEAD THE *PROJECT STEVE* SCIENTISTS, WHO NOW NUMBER MORE THAN *1,200*, STATE:

EVOLUTION IS A VITAL, WELL-SUPPORTED, UNIFYING PRINCIPLE OF THE BIOLOGICAL SCIENCES, AND THE SCIENTIFIC EVIDENCE IS OVERWHELMINGLY IN FAVOR OF THE IDEA THAT ALL LIVING THINGS SHARE A COMMON ANCESTRY. ALTHOUGH THERE ARE LEGITIMATE DEBATES ABOUT THE PATTERNS AND PROCESSES OF EVOLUTION, THERE IS NO SERIOUS SCIENTIFIC DOUBT THAT EVOLUTION OCCURRED OR THAT NATURAL SELECTION IS A MAJOR MECHANISM IN ITS OCCURRENCE. IT IS SCIENTIFICALLY INAPPROPRIATE AND PEDAGOGICALLY IRRESPONSIBLE FOR CREATIONIST PSEUDOSCIENCE, INCLUDING BUT NOT LIMITED TO 'INTELLIGENT DESIGN', TO BE INTRODUCED INTO THE SCIENCE CURRICULA OF OUR NATION'S PUBLIC SCHOOLS.

SOME RELIGIOUS FOLK ALSO NOTE A POINT THEY CONSIDER GOES AGAINST EVOLUTION: *THAT WE LIVE IN A UNIVERSE THAT IS PERFECT FOR LIFE.*

SCIENTISTS CONSIDER THAT EVEN THE *TINIEST* VARIATION OF ANY ONE OF A VARIETY OF ELEMENTS WOULD MAKE THIS WORLD *IMPOSSIBLE* FOR US TO SURVIVE ON. SO SURELY *GOD* MADE IT LIKE THIS ON PURPOSE - A *TAILOR-MADE WORLD, JUST FOR US!*

HOWEVER, SOME *NON-RELIGIOUS* PEOPLE NOTE THAT A BETTER PROOF OF GOD WOULD BE THE OPPOSITE – IF WE LIVED IN A UNIVERSE THAT DID *NOT* SUPPORT LIFE...

...AND GOD INTERVENED TO ALLOW US TO SURVIVE IN SUCH AN INHOSPITABLE ENVIRONMENT.

ROY SPECKHARDT, OF THE AMERICAN HUMANIST ASSOCIATION, GIVES US HIS OPINION:

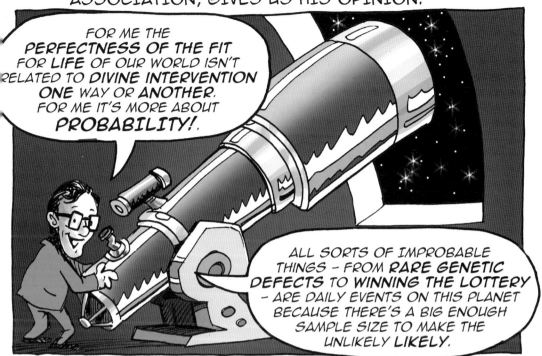

FOR ME THE **PERFECTNESS OF THE FIT** FOR **LIFE** OF OUR WORLD ISN'T RELATED TO **DIVINE INTERVENTION** ONE WAY OR ANOTHER. FOR ME IT'S MORE ABOUT **PROBABILITY!**.

ALL SORTS OF IMPROBABLE THINGS – FROM **RARE GENETIC DEFECTS** TO **WINNING THE LOTTERY** – ARE DAILY EVENTS ON THIS PLANET BECAUSE THERE'S A BIG ENOUGH SAMPLE SIZE TO MAKE THE UNLIKELY **LIKELY**.

WHILE IT'S **HIGHLY IMPROBABLE** THAT A WORLD LIKE OURS COULD SUPPORT LIFE, LOOKING AT OUR GALAXY'S **300 BILLION** SOLAR SYSTEMS, IT BECOMES LIKELY THAT AT LEAST **ONE** WORLD LIKE OURS WOULD OCCUR.

AND THINKING ABOUT THE **100 BILLION GALAXIES** IN THE UNIVERSE, EACH WITH **HUNDREDS OF BILLIONS** OF SOLAR SYSTEMS, WITH MANY MORE PLANETS... THEN, OF COURSE, THE IMPROBABLE CONDITIONS WILL EXIST ON **AT LEAST ONE** PLANET... YOU DON'T NEED **GOD** WHEN YOU HAVE ENORMOUS SAMPLE SIZES LIKE THAT!

SUCH RATIONAL EXPLANATIONS ARE TO BE ENCOURAGED, BUT THE IRRATIONAL *'BELIEF SYSTEMS'* THAT RELIGIONS OFTEN ENCOURAGE DO NOT HELP RATIONAL THINKING. *STEPHEN LAW* HAS OUTLINED *EIGHT MECHANISMS* BY WHICH SUCH SYSTEMS, IN BOTH *MAINSTREAM RELIGIONS* AND IN VARIOUS *NEW AGE PRACTICES*, ARE INTRODUCED AND PROMOTED...

1. *PLAYING THE MYSTERY CARD*
2. *'BUT IT FITS!'*
   AND THE BLUNDERBUSS OF CRAP
3. *MOVING THE GOAL POSTS*
4. *GOING NUCLEAR*
5. *'I JUST KNOW!'*
6. *PSEUDO-PROFUNDITY*
7. *THE AMAZINGLY PERSUASIVE POWER OF ACCUMULATED ANECDOTE (TAPPAA)*
8. *PRESSING YOUR BUTTONS*

STEPHENLAW.BLOGSPOT.COM

WHILE MY BOOK CONTAINS MANY RELIGIOUS EXAMPLES – FROM *YOUNG EARTH CREATIONISM* TO *CHRISTIAN SCIENCE* – ACTUALLY I'M NOT ARGUING THAT ALL RELIGIOUS BELIEF SYSTEMS ARE ESSENTIALLY IRRATIONAL.

SEVERAL RECENT BOOKS HAVE DONE THAT, INCLUDING BOOKS BY *CHRISTOPHER HITCHENS*, *SAM HARRIS* AND *RICHARD DAWKINS*. ALL THREE ARGUE THAT THE CONTENT OF RELIGIOUS BELIEF GENERALLY IS NOT JUST *NONSENSE*, BUT *DANGEROUS NONSENSE*.

MY AIM WITH THE *BELIEVING BULLSHIT* BOOK IS *DIFFERENT*. IT'S NOT THE CONTENT OF RELIGIOUS BELIEF THAT I CRITICIZE, BUT THE MANNER IN WHICH *RELIGIOUS BELIEF SYSTEMS* ARE SOMETIMES DEFENDED AND PROMOTED.

NOW LET'S TAKE A LOOK AT SOME OF STEPHEN'S *EIGHT MECHANISMS* BY WHICH BELIEF SYSTEMS ARE PROMOTED:

PLAYING THE MYSTERY CARD.

OH DEAR, MR RELIGION – YOUR BELIEF SYSTEM LOOKS *PRETTY IRRATIONAL.*

NOT ONLY DO YOU HAVE *LITTLE* IN THE WAY OF ARGUMENT FOR WHAT YOU BELIEVE, THERE ALSO SEEMS TO BE *POWERFUL EVIDENCE* AGAINST IT!

BUT YOU WANT TO *CONVINCE* YOURSELF AND OTHERS THAT YOUR BELIEFS ARE *NOT NEARLY* AS RIDICULOUS AS THEY SEEM.

HMM, A TOUGH JOB! WHAT DO YOU SAY?

BUT, BUT... IT'S BEYOND *SCIENCE* OR *REASON* TO DECIDE!!!

AH, MR RELIGION... YA GOT ME THERE.

THIS *'PLAYING THE MYSTERY CARD'* INVOLVES MAKING YOUR BELIEFS *IMMUNE* TO BEING REFUTED BY SOME *UNJUSTIFIED APPEAL* TO *MYSTERY*. THE MOST POPULAR VERSION OF THIS STRATEGY IS FOR BELIEVERS TO SAY:

WE MUST ACKNOWLEDGE THAT *SCIENCE* AND *REASON* HAVE THEIR LIMITS.

IT IS *SHEER ARROGANCE* TO SUPPOSE THEY CAN EXPLAIN EVERYTHING.

AH, THE SUPPOSED *ARROGANCE OF SCIENCE!* SCIENTISTS PUT FORWARD THEORIES AS HYPOTHESES, TEST THEM, AND REGULARLY CHANGE THEIR MINDS WHEN THEIR THEORIES ARE FALSIFIED. YET THE SCIENTIFIC COMMUNITY IS OFTEN ACCUSED OF *ARROGANCE*.

IS IT ANY *LESS* ARROGANT WHEN RELIGIOUS LEADERS CLAIM TO KNOW ANSWERS WITH *CERTAINTY* AND INSIST NOTHING *CAN* OR *WOULD EVER* CHANGE THEIR MINDS?

'QUESTIONING INQUIRY'

'UNQUESTIONED AUTHORITY'

WHICH SEEMS MORE ARROGANT TO YOU, DEAR READER?

BUT BACK TO THE IDEA THAT SCIENCE CAN'T EXPLAIN EVERYTHING - *YES, AGREED.* BUT *SO WHAT?*

PHILOSOPHER *DAVID HUME* FAMOUSLY NOTED THAT...

...SCIENCE ULTIMATELY REVEALS ONLY *WHAT IS THE CASE.* IT CANNOT TELL US WHAT WE MORALLY *OUGHT* OR *OUGHT NOT* TO DO.

NOR, IT SEEMS, CAN SCIENCE EXPLAIN *WHY* THE UNIVERSE ITSELF EXISTS - WHY THERE IS *ANYTHING AT ALL.* SCIENTIFIC EXPLANATIONS INVOLVE APPEALING TO *NATURAL CAUSES OR LAWS.*

FOR EXAMPLE, IF YOU ASK *WHY* THE WATER FROZE IN THE PIPES LAST NIGHT.

A SCIENTIST MIGHT EXPLAIN BY POINTING OUT THAT THE TEMPERATURE OF THE WATER FELL *BELOW ZERO,* AND THAT IT IS A *LAW OF NATURE* THAT WATER FREEZES *BELOW ZERO.*

THAT WOULD EXPLAIN WHY THE WATER FROZE. BUT WHAT EXPLAINS *WHY* THERE ARE *ANY* NATURAL LAWS OR CAUSES IN THE FIRST PLACE?

WHAT EXPLAINS *WHY* THERE IS A NATURAL WORLD AT ALL? WHY THERE IS *SOMETHING* RATHER THAN *NOTHING?* HERE, IT WOULD SEEM, SCIENCE CANNOT PROVIDE ANSWERS.

BUT BECAUSE THERE PROBABLY ARE QUESTIONS THAT SCIENCE **CANNOT** ANSWER, IT DOES NOT FOLLOW THAT SCIENCE (AND REASON) CANNOT ESTABLISH **BEYOND REASONABLE DOUBT** THAT CERTAIN SUPERNATURAL PHENOMENA **DO** OR **DON'T** EXIST.

SCIENCE CAN PRETTY CONCLUSIVELY RULE OUT AT LEAST **SOME** CLAIMS OF A SUPERNATURAL NATURE. THAT IS BECAUSE, WHILE SUCH CLAIMS MAY CONCERN THE **UNOBSERVABLE**, THE CLAIMS NEVERTHELESS HAVE **OBSERVABLE CONSEQUENCES**.

THAT MAKES SUCH CLAIMS **TESTABLE**. WE CAN **CONSTRUCT** VARIOUS TESTS TO INVESTIGATE **SUPERNATURAL CLAIMS**.

THEY ARE, IN THIS RESPECT, NO DIFFERENT TO HYPOTHESES CONCERNING **OTHER** 'HIDDEN' PHENOMENA, SUCH AS TINY, UNOBSERVABLE PARTICLES...

IT'S NO GOOD — ELECTRONS ARE JUST TOO SMALL TO OBSERVE.

ELECTRONS MAY NOT BE OBSERVABLE, BUT WE CAN **PREDICT** AND **LOOK FOR** THEIR EFFECTS.

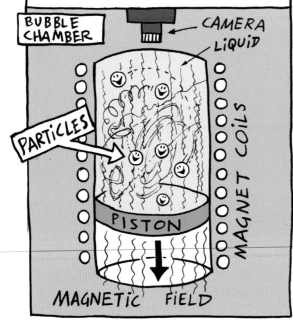

BUBBLE CHAMBER
CAMERA
LIQUID
PARTICLES
MAGNET COILS
PISTON
MAGNETIC FIELD

OR THE **DISTANT PAST** OF THIS PLANET.

TAKE FOR EXAMPLE THE RESEARCH DONE BY PROFESSOR **CHRISTOPHER FRENCH**, **LYN WILLIAMS** AND **HAYLEY O'DONNELL** AT GOLDSMITHS, UNIVERSITY OF LONDON.

THEY CONDUCTED A STUDY INTO THE CLAIM THAT **CRYSTALS** HAVE **UNUSUAL POWERS** THAT CAN BE DETECTED WHEN THEY ARE **HELD**. THE STUDY COMPARED THE REACTIONS OF A GROUP OF VOLUNTEERS WHO WERE TOLD TO MEDITATE WHILE CLUTCHING **REAL CRYSTALS** BOUGHT FROM 'NEW AGE' SHOPS, WITH A CONTROL GROUP GIVEN **FAKE** CRYSTALS

THOSE GIVEN **REAL** CRYSTALS REPORTED **HIGHER CONCENTRATION POWERS, HEIGHTENED ENERGY LEVELS** AND **BETTER SPIRITUAL WELL-BEING.**

REAL CRYSTALS

FAKE CRYSTALS

HOWEVER, **EXACTLY THE SAME FEELINGS** WERE REPORTED BY THOSE HOLDING **FAKE** CRYSTALS!

THEY DID NOT FIND **ANY DIFFERENCE** IN THE EFFECTS REPORTED BETWEEN **REAL** AND **FAKE**. THIS SUGGESTS THAT THE POWER OF CRYSTALS IS IN THE **MIND** RATHER THAN IN THE **CRYSTALS THEMSELVES.**

IF YOU BELIEVED IN THE MIRACULOUS POWERS OF CRYSTALS BUT WERE PRESENTED WITH EXPERIMENTAL RESULTS THAT INDICATED OTHERWISE, THEN HOW WOULD YOU REACT? PERHAPS SOMETHING LIKE THIS:

THERE IS *MUCH* THAT EXISTS *BEYOND* THE VISIBLE SPECTRUM OF LIGHT, AND *BEYOND* THE FIVE SENSES. NOT BEING ABLE TO *PROVE* THE EXISTENCE OF SOMETHING DOES NOT *DISPROVE* ITS EXISTENCE.

MUCH IS YET TO BE DISCOVERED...

YOU WOULD DO *BETTER* TO DISCOVER IT BY LOOKING *OUTSIDE YOUR NARROW FRAME* OF REFERENCE.

THE FIRST THREE THINGS SHE SAYS ARE, OF COURSE, ALL TRUE. BUT WHAT ABOUT REACTING TO THE *ACTUAL EXPERIMENT?* IT MAKES SPECIFIC POINTS WHICH THE LADY DOES NOT ADDRESS AT ALL.

THE EXPERIMENT PRODUCED SOME STRONG EVIDENCE THAT *SOME* OF THE EFFECTS ARE *NOT* A RESULT OF SOME *SPECIAL FEATURE* OF THE CRYSTALS, BUT *OTHER ASPECTS,* LIKE THE *POWER OF SUGGESTION.*

WHAT WE HAVE HERE IS NOT A MERE *ABSENCE OF EVIDENCE* FOR THE CLAIM THAT CRYSTALS HAVE SUCH EFFECTS, BUT SOME *POSITIVE EVIDENCE* OF THE *ABSENCE* OF ANY SUCH EFFECTS.

SHE *DOESN'T* ANSWER THAT POINT.

IT OFTEN SEEMS TO BE MERELY A **COMBINATION** OF SUCH **GUT FEELING** AND **INTUITION**... AND A HEAVY RELIANCE ON VARIOUS ANECDOTES ABOUT THE EFFECTS OF SUPERNATURAL PHENOMENA.

THERE DOESN'T SEEM MUCH REASON TO
THINK THE SCIENTIFIC METHOD IS NOT
SUITABLE FOR INVESTIGATING THE ALLEGED
POWERS OF SUPERNATURAL PHENOMENA.

IN FACT, MANY OF
THE CLAIMS MADE
ABOUT SUCH
SUPERNATURAL
PHENOMENA *ARE*
SCIENTIFICALLY
INVESTIGABLE,
BECAUSE, AS
NOTED,
THEY HAVE
OBSERVABLE,
EMPIRICALLY
TESTABLE
CONSEQUENCES.
SCIENCE HAS
PRODUCED GOOD
EVIDENCE THAT
MANY OF THESE
CLAIMS ARE
FALSE.

SO, I FIND IT RATHER
ANNOYING WHEN SOME BELIEVER
IN SUPERNATURAL CLAIMS, IN
RESPONSE TO A SCIENTIFIC
REFUTATION OF WHAT THEY
BELIEVE, ENTIRELY IGNORES
THE ARGUMENT.

INSTEAD THEY
ACCUSE THEIR
CRITIC OF
SCIENTISM,
AND START
RECITING
THE OLD, WEAK,
MANTRA:

AH, BUT
THIS IS
BEYOND THE
ABILITY OF
SCIENCE TO
DETERMINE.

ERR...

SOME THINGS PROBABLY ARE BEYOND THE ABILITY OF *SCIENCE*
OR EVEN *REASON*, TO SETTLE. BUT THAT DOES NOT MEAN *ALL*
SUPERNATURAL CLAIMS ARE. MANY HAVE BEEN TESTED
AND FOUND TO BE *FALSE*.

NOW ANOTHER OF STEPHEN LAW'S MECHANISMS BY WHICH A BELIEF SYSTEM IS INTRODUCED AND PROMOTED: *'BUT IT FITS!'*

THIS INVOLVES COMING UP WITH VARIOUS WAYS, OFTEN VERY ELABORATE, OF MAKING *EVIDENCE* AND *THEORY 'FIT'* AFTER ALL – DESPITE MANY INDICATIONS THAT THEY DON'T! WE SAW SOMETHING OF THAT EARLIER ON, WITH DAVE AND HIS ALIEN DOGS.

HERE'S *STEPHEN* TO TELL US MORE:

I THINK THAT THE KEY THING IN TERMS OF PUBLIC UNDERSTANDING IS GETTING PEOPLE *IMMUNIZED* AGAINST THE SEDUCTIVE THOUGHT THAT IF YOU CAN MAKE *YOUR* THEORY CONSISTENT WITH THE EVIDENCE... THEN IT IS AS WELL CONFIRMED AS *ANY OTHER* THEORY CONSISTENT WITH THE EVIDENCE.

CREATIONISTS WORK ON SHOWING HOW *THEIR* THEORY 'FITS' THE EVIDENCE.

WHICH SOUNDS LIKE WHAT *SCIENTISTS* DO, RIGHT? – DEVELOP THEORIES TO 'FIT' THE EVIDENCE.

BOING!

IN FACT, THAT'S *NOT* WHAT SCIENTISTS DO...

JUST GETTING THAT CLEAR WOULD BE A HUGE STEP FORWARD...

THE KEY POINT IS THAT ANY THEORY, NO MATTER HOW ABSURD IT IS, CAN BE MADE CONSISTENT WITH EVIDENCE, MADE TO 'FIT'. BUT THAT IS **NOT** WHAT SCIENCE ACTUALLY DOES OR REQUIRES. SCIENCE REQUIRES CERTAIN CONDITIONS IN ORDER FOR A THEORY TO BE STRONGLY CONFIRMED BY EVIDENCE. TO BEGIN WITH, THE THEORY MUST MAKE PREDICTIONS THAT ARE:

CLEAR AND PRECISE
SURPRISING
TRUE

GOING INTO THIS MORE: FROM A THEORY WE CAN HOPEFULLY DERIVE PREDICTIONS ABOUT THINGS THAT WE CAN OBSERVE.

FOR EXAMPLE, THE PREDICTION: **'ALL RAVENS ARE BLACK'.** WE CAN PREDICT THAT THE NEXT RAVEN TO FLY BY WILL BE BLACK, AND WE CAN OBSERVE THAT.

THEREFORE, BECAUSE IT SAYS SOMETHING ABOUT THE *OBSERVABLE*, IT MEANS THE THEORY CAN BE *TESTED*. WE CAN CHECK IF PREDICTIONS COMING FROM THAT THEORY ARE TRUE.

ALSO, IT'S IMPORTANT TO NOTE THAT IT'S A MATTER OF *DEGREE* - A THEORY IS CONFIRMED BY EVIDENCE TO DIFFERENT DEGREES, STRONGER OR WEAKER. JUST *ONE* BLACK RAVEN FLYING BY GIVES US *SOME* LEVEL OF CONFIRMATION OF OUR PREDICTION *'ALL RAVENS ARE BLACK'* - BUT NOT MUCH. WE NEED *MORE* THAN THAT FOR STRONG CONFIRMATION.

IN ANY CASE, IT'S USUALLY *NOT* LIKE NEWSPAPERS OFTEN PUT IT - THAT SOMETHING IS DEFINITELY PROVEN, THE END, THAT'S IT, FIXED FOREVER...

A THEORY CAN BE STRONGLY CONFIRMED IF, FROM IT, WE CAN DERIVE PREDICTIONS THAT ARE CLEAR AND PRECISE. IF OUR PREDICTION IS VERY VAGUE, LIKE *'IT WILL RAIN SOON'* WITHOUT OUR DEFINING WHAT *'SOON'* MEANS... THEN WHEN THE PREDICTION APPEARS TO BE FALSE IT WILL BE PRETTY EASY TO CLAIM: *'OH, I DIDN'T MEAN TODAY!'*

AND THE PREDICTION ALSO NEEDS TO BE **SURPRISING**. PREDICT SOMETHING THAT IS QUITE LIKELY TO HAPPEN ANYWAY, EVEN IF YOUR THEORY IS NOT TRUE, AND YOUR THEORY IS NOT STRONGLY CONFIRMED BY THE PREDICTION'S BEING TRUE.

Part 2

Science and Religion

DING DING!

SO, NOW LET'S MOVE OUT TO SOME WIDER CONSIDERATIONS OF SCIENCE AND RELIGION IN GENERAL.

AND WE'VE GOT A TEAM OF 'ATHEIST ALL-STARS' TO HELP US OUT A BIT.

HERE'S THE FIRST - CHRISTOPHER HITCHENS - TAKING PART IN A DEBATE...

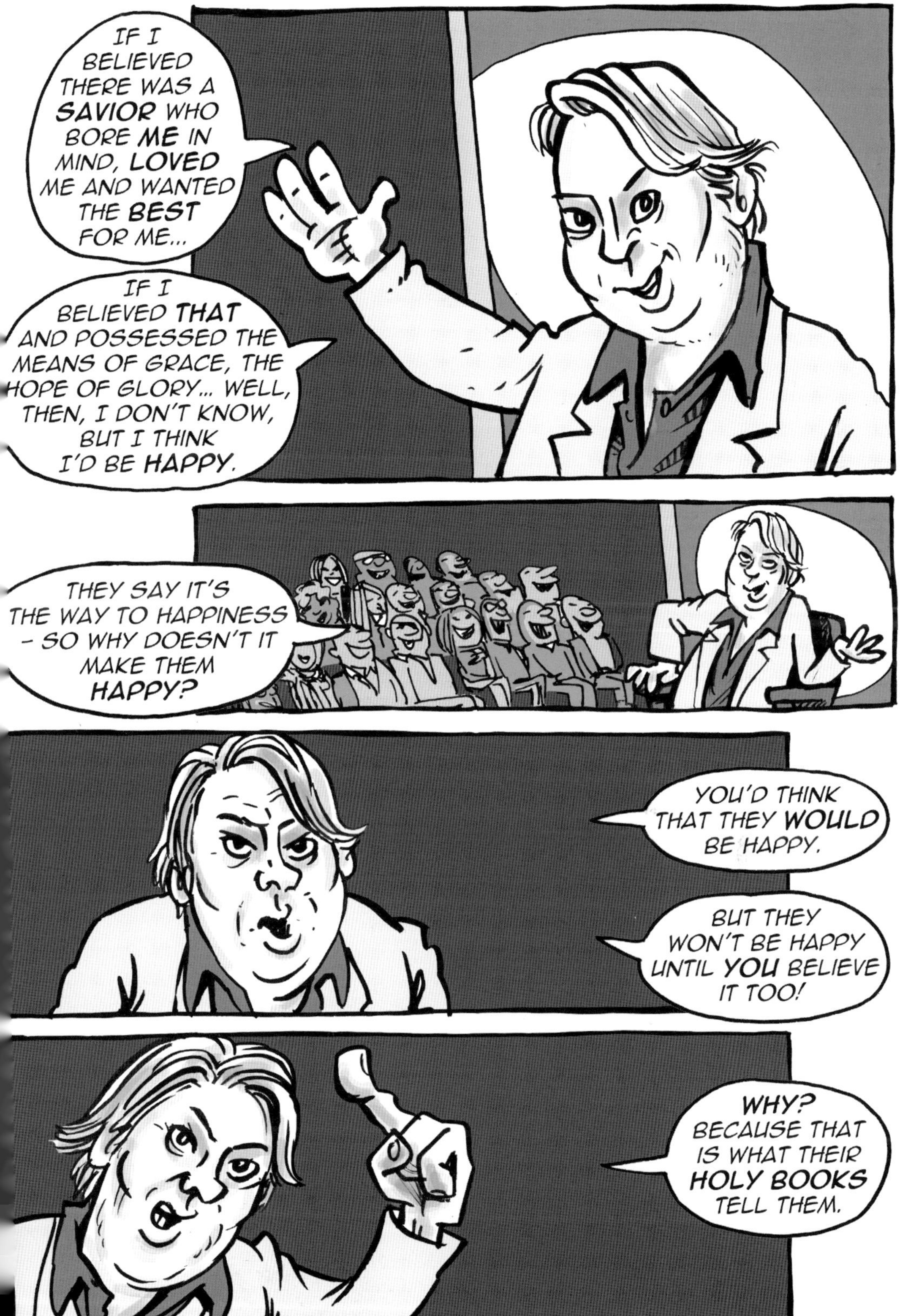
IF I BELIEVED THERE WAS A SAVIOR WHO BORE ME IN MIND, LOVED ME AND WANTED THE BEST FOR ME...
IF I BELIEVED THAT AND POSSESSED THE MEANS OF GRACE, THE HOPE OF GLORY... WELL, THEN, I DON'T KNOW, BUT I THINK I'D BE HAPPY.
THEY SAY IT'S THE WAY TO HAPPINESS - SO WHY DOESN'T IT MAKE THEM HAPPY?
YOU'D THINK THAT THEY WOULD BE HAPPY.
BUT THEY WON'T BE HAPPY UNTIL YOU BELIEVE IT TOO!
WHY? BECAUSE THAT IS WHAT THEIR HOLY BOOKS TELL THEM.

SO, HERE WE HAVE A KEY POINT, MADE IN THE USUAL FORCEFUL AND IRONIC FASHION OF HITCHENS.

RELIGIOUS PEOPLE, WHETHER CHRISTIAN, JEWISH, MUSLIM AND OTHERS, SOMEHOW DON'T SEEM TO BE MADE VERY HAPPY BY THE GREAT SITUATION THEY CLAIM TO BE IN. IT'S A BASIC ELEMENT OF PSYCHOLOGY THAT SEEMS TO REVEAL A LOT.

SHOULDN'T THEY BE GOING AROUND ALL DAY IN A STATE OF *BLISS*? BATHING IN THE GRACE OF GOD?

INSTEAD THEY SEEM TO SPEND MOST OF THEIR TIME INSECURE...

COMPLAINING...

OR GETTING ANNOYED.

QUITE OFTEN *VIOLENTLY SO!*

KEY TEXTS OF VARIOUS RELIGIONS INDICATE THAT PEOPLE WHO DON'T BELIEVE THAT FORM OF RELIGION ARE, TO PUT IT MILDLY, LESS THAN DESIRABLE AND SHOULD BE DEALT WITH VIOLENTLY. HOW ABOUT THIS LITTLE LOT, FOR EXAMPLE:

IF YOUR VERY OWN BROTHER, OR YOUR SON OR DAUGHTER, OR THE WIFE YOU LOVE, OR YOUR CLOSEST FRIEND SECRETLY ENTICES YOU, SAYING: LET US GO AND WORSHIP OTHER GODS...

DO NOT YIELD TO HIM OR LISTEN TO HIM! SHOW HIM NO PITY. DO NOT SPARE HIM OR SHIELD HIM!

YOU MUST CERTAINLY PUT HIM TO DEATH!

*DEUTERONOMY 13:6-9

THE INFIDELS ARE YOUR SWORN ENEMIES!

PROPHET, MAKE WAR ON THE INFIDELS!!!

QUR'AN: SURA 4:101 AND SURA 66:9

IT HAS NOW BEEN SOME 400 YEARS THAT A HORRENDOUS ZIONIST CLAN HAS BEEN RULING THE MAJOR WORLD AFFAIRS... THEY ARE BEHIND THE SCENES OF THE MAJOR POWER CIRCLES IN POLITICAL, MEDIA, MONETARY, AND BANKING ORGANIZATIONS IN THE WORLD!

MAHMOUD AHMADINEJAD, PRESIDENT OF IRAN, 2005-13:

AND WE DON'T HAVE TO LOOK FAR FOR EXAMPLES, SOMETIMES EXTREME ONES, OF RELIGIOUS LAWS BEING *SO STRICTLY ENFORCED* THAT THE CONSEQUENCES ARE HORRIBLE, EVEN *HORRIFIC*. AND WHY ARE *SO MANY OF THEM* AGAINST *WOMEN*?

SAUDI ARABIA IN 2002 – A SCHOOL IN MECCA CATCHES FIRE, WITH 800 PUPILS INSIDE.

STOP! YOU CAN'T GO OUT *IMPROPERLY DRESSED!*

RELIGIOUS POLICEMEN STOPPED THE GIRLS FROM GETTING OUT AS THEY WERE 'IMPROPERLY DRESSED'– NOT WEARING THE HEADSCARVES AND ABAYAS (BLACK ROBES) REQUIRED BY THE KINGDOM'S STRICT INTERPRETATION OF ISLAM.

THE MUCH-FEARED RELIGIOUS POLICE, KNOWN AS *MUTAWEEN* OR FORMALLY AS 'THE COMMISSION FOR THE PROMOTION OF VIRTUE AND PREVENTION OF VICE', EVEN STOPPED MEN WHO TRIED TO HELP THE GIRLS.

AS A RESULT, *15* SCHOOLGIRLS DIED IN THE FIRE. ALL BECAUSE THE RELIGION SAID THEY WERE *'IMPROPERLY ATTIRED'*.

IN ISRAEL SOME EXTREME ORTHODOX JEWS ENFORCE DRESS AND BEHAVIOR CODES, IN AGGRESSIVE WAYS THAT *HARASS* AND *PUNISH* PEOPLE WHO CHOOSE TO LIVE THEIR LIVES IN A DIFFERENT WAY THAT IS DEEMED *UNACCEPTABLE* BY THE RELIGION.

FOR EXAMPLE, IN THE DEVOUTLY RELIGIOUS CITY OF *BEIT SHEMESH*, NEAR JERUSALEM, ULTRA-ORTHODOX JEWS HAVE ATTACKED SEVERAL BUSES OVER A DISPUTE ABOUT WOMEN NOT SITTING IN THEIR 'PROPER PLACE' - *AT THE BACK!*

THERE ARE SPECIAL *'MEHADRIN'* BUS LINES DEDICATED TO ORTHODOX JEWS, ON WHICH MEN AND WOMEN SIT SEPARATELY, ON A *VOLUNTARY* BASIS.

BUT SOME DON'T SEEM KEEN ON THE *'VOLUNTARY'* PART!

AND MUCH AS ORTHODOX MUSLIM 'POLICE' HARASS PEOPLE ON THE STREETS OF SAUDI ARABIA, ORTHODOX JEWS ROAM THE STREETS IN SOME ISRAELI CITIES, 'SUPERVISING' THE SABBATH.

OR DRESS CODES. ESPECIALLY WHAT WOMEN CHOOSE TO WEAR!

AND WHEN RELIGIOUS RULES LEAD TO SUCH *INTOLERANCE* TOWARDS PEOPLE OF YOUR *OWN* GROUP, IT'S NO WONDER THAT IT CAN OFTEN ENCOURAGE *OUTRIGHT HOSTILITY* TO THOSE OF ANOTHER.

THIS CAN LEAD TO A SITUATION WHERE RELIGION PUSHES PEOPLE INTO ACTS OF EXTREME CRUELTY.

OF COURSE, 'MODERATE' RELIGIOUS PEOPLE OFTEN SAY THAT THE OLD TEXTS DON'T HAVE TO BE TAKEN LITERALLY OR FOLLOWED SLAVISHLY WITHOUT ADJUSTING TO THE MODERN WORLD. MANY MODERATE MUSLIMS STATE THAT SUCH QUOTES FROM THE QUR'AN SHOULD BE SEEN IN THEIR HISTORICAL CONTEXT AND ARE MISUNDERSTOOD.

ACTUALLY, THE QUR'AN TEACHES US TO **RESPECT** A PERSON'S **FREEDOM OF CHOICE** TO BE A DISBELIEVER.

QUR'AN 18:29 PROCLAIMS: **'THE TRUTH IS FROM YOUR LORD'**, MEANING IT'S THE **FREE WILL** OF ANY PERSON TO BELIEVE IN GOD OR NOT – AND ONLY **GOD** CAN JUDGE THEM.

HERE'S ANOTHER OF OUR FRIENDS, **ROY SPECKHARDT**, OF THE **AMERICAN HUMANIST ASSOCIATION:**

JUST ABOUT **ALL THE ANCIENT** TEXTS OF SUPPOSED DIVINE REVELATION SAY **GHASTLY THINGS** THAT ARE ANTITHETICAL TO EMPATHETIC APPROACHES TO HUMANITY.

FORTUNATELY, JUST AS MOST **US** CATHOLICS IGNORE THE POPE'S BAN ON CONTRACEPTIVES, SO CAN MANY MUSLIMS WORLDWIDE REINTERPRET THE QUR'AN IN A **MORE HUMANIST** WAY IF THEY SO WISH.

WE **APPRECIATE** AND **SUPPORT** THE MANY MODERATE AND PROGRESSIVE MUSLIMS THAT STRIVE FOR **PEACE** AND **POSITIVE CHANGE** WITHIN ISLAM... CHANGE IN THE ISLAMIST REGIMES **HAS** TO OCCUR WITH BROAD SUPPORT WITHIN THEM, NOT JUST EXTERNAL CRITICISM.

A KEY RELATED POINT IS THAT IF SUCH MODERATES ADJUST THEIR RELIGION ACCORDING TO THE MODERN WORLD, THEN BY WHAT STANDARD? WHAT OTHER MODEL DO THEY USE TO REASSESS THE OLD PRACTICES THAT USED TO BE FINE?

IT USED TO BE OK TO ENSLAVE BLACK PEOPLE, BUT NOW IT'S NOT.

IT USED TO BE OK TO KNOCK THE HELL OUT OF YOUR EIGHT-YEAR-OLD DAUGHTER, BUT NOW IT'S NOT.

SURELY IT'S *HUMANIST* AND *SCIENTIFIC* IDEALS THAT DRIVE THAT EFFORT AT REASSESSMENT OF SUCH OLD PRACTICES?

SO, WHAT IS *HUMANISM*? WELL, LET'S HEAR FROM SOME OTHER INTERESTING FOLK ON THAT:

ALBERT EINSTEIN – SCIENTIST, NOBEL PRIZEWINNER IN PHYSICS, ORIGINATOR OF THE THEORY OF RELATIVITY...

SCIENCE HAS BEEN CHARGED WITH UNDERMINING MORALITY, BUT THE CHARGE IS *UNJUST*. A MAN'S ETHICAL BEHAVIOR SHOULD BE BASED EFFECTUALLY ON *SYMPATHY*, *EDUCATION*, AND *SOCIAL TIES* AND *NEEDS*; NO RELIGIOUS BASIS IS NECESSARY.

MAN WOULD INDEED BE IN A *POOR WAY* IF HE HAD TO BE RESTRAINED BY FEAR OF PUNISHMENT AND HOPE OF REWARD AFTER DEATH!

ISAAC ASIMOV – SCIENTIST, AUTHOR, AND PAST PRESIDENT OF THE AMERICAN HUMANIST ASSOCIATION

ALBERT SCHWEITZER, ACCEPTING THE NOBEL PEACE PRIZE IN 1952.

HUMANISM, IN ALL ITS SIMPLICITY, IS THE ONLY GENUINE SPIRITUALITY.

HUMANISTS RECOGNIZE THAT IT IS ONLY WHEN PEOPLE FEEL FREE TO THINK FOR THEMSELVES, USING *REASON* AS THEIR GUIDE... THAT THEY ARE BEST CAPABLE OF DEVELOPING *VALUES* THAT SUCCEED IN SATISFYING HUMAN NEEDS AND SERVING HUMAN INTERESTS!.

GLORIA STEINEM – FOUNDER OF *MS*.MAGAZINE, HUMANIST PIONEER AWARDEE.

WHEN WE SPEAK OF *EQUALITY*, OF WOMEN AND MEN, OF BLACKS AND WHITES, OF ALL THE WORLD'S PEOPLE, WE ARE TALKING ABOUT *HUMANISM*.

HTTP://AMERICANHUMANIST.ORG/HUMANISM

THE AMERICAN HUMANIST ASSOCIATION TELLS US THIS:
'KURT VONNEGUT, WHO SERVED FOR MANY YEARS AS THE AHA'S
HONORARY PRESIDENT, SAID IT MOST SUCCINCTLY:

If you need the threat of eternal torture in order to be a good person YOU'RE NOT A GOOD PERSON.

...BEING A **HUMANIST** MEANS TRYING TO BEHAVE **DECENTLY** WITHOUT EXPECTATION OF **REWARDS** OR **PUNISHMENT** AFTER YOU ARE DEAD.

'HUMANISM IS A WORLDVIEW WHICH SAYS THAT REASON AND SCIENCE ARE THE BEST WAYS TO UNDERSTAND THE WORLD AROUND US, AND THAT DIGNITY AND COMPASSION SHOULD BE THE BASIS FOR HOW YOU ACT TOWARD SOMEONE ELSE.'

AMERICAN HUMANIST ASSOCIATION
GOOD WITHOUT A GOD

'HUMANISM IS NONTHEISTIC. BY THIS, WE DON'T MEAN TO SAY THAT THERE IS NO GOD. INSTEAD, WE SAY THAT THERE IS NO PROOF FOR THE EXISTENCE OF GOD, ANY GODS, THE SUPERNATURAL OR AN AFTERLIFE... THEREFORE, WE TAKE VERY SERIOUSLY THE IDEA THAT "NO DEITY WILL SAVE US; WE MUST SAVE OURSELVES". WE ARE LIVING THE ONLY LIFE WE'LL HAVE, IN THE ONLY WORLD WE KNOW ABOUT. THE RESPONSIBILITY FOR THE CHOICES WE MAKE ARE OURS AND OURS ALONE.'

NO GOD?
...NO PROBLEM!

Be **good**
for **goodness'** sake.
Humanism is the idea that you can be good without a belief in God.

HERE'S **HITCHENS** AGAIN, STATING WHAT HE THINKS WOULD BE A REASONABLE STATE OF EXISTENCE FOR RELIGIONS IN SOCIETY, FOR A STATE OF PEACE BETWEEN THE RELIGIOUS AND THE HUMANISTS.

ANOTHER POINT OFTEN MADE WHEN SCIENTISTS OR ATHEISTS CRITICIZE RELIGION IS:

WHY NOT JUST LET THE RELIGIOUS *ENJOY* THAT SENSE OF *HOPE* IT GIVES THEM?

WE *NEED* A SENSE OF HOPE, DON'T WE?

ANOTHER OF OUR KEY FIGURES, *RICHARD DAWKINS*, MAKES THE POINT THAT THE UNIVERSE DOES NOT OWE US A SENSE OF HOPE! IT COULD BE THAT THE UNIVERSE IS A *TOTALLY HOPELESS PLACE*... AND, IF IT IS, IT'S *ILLOGICAL* TO SAY THAT THIS GIVES YOU EVIDENCE FOR BELIEF IN GOD.

YOU ARE HERE

I PERSONALLY *DON'T* THINK THE UNIVERSE IS A HOPELESS PLACE..

BUT YOU *CANNOT* SAY THIS:

I BELIEVE IN GOD, BECAUSE THAT GIVES ME HOPE!

WE SHOULD SAY: 'I BELIEVE IN X BECAUSE THERE IS *SOME EVIDENCE* FOR X'.

AND THERE IS NOT A *TINY SHRED* OF EVIDENCE FOR THE EXISTENCE OF *ANY* GOD.

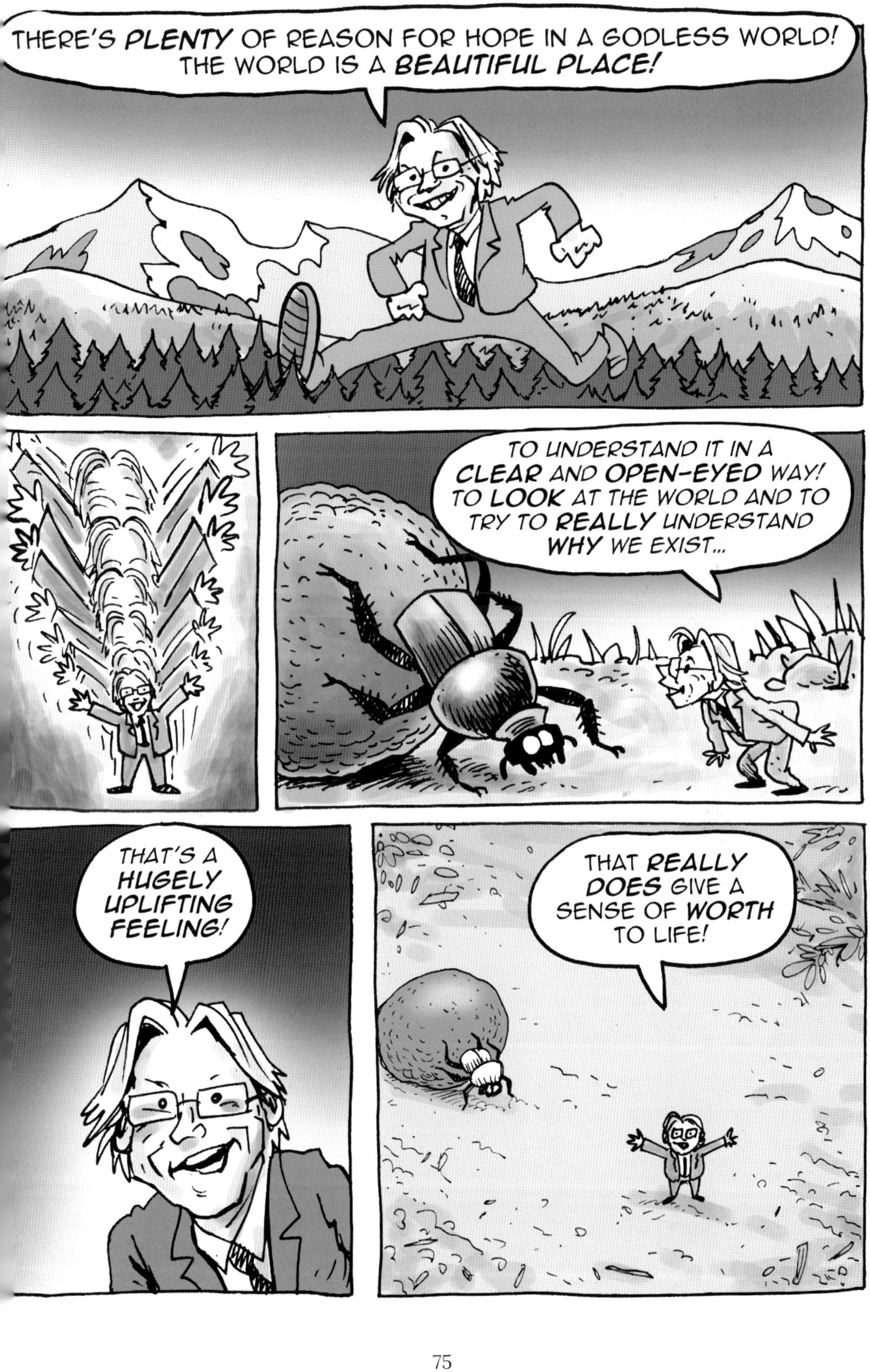
THERE'S PLENTY OF REASON FOR HOPE IN A GODLESS WORLD! THE WORLD IS A BEAUTIFUL PLACE!
TO UNDERSTAND IT IN A CLEAR AND OPEN-EYED WAY! TO LOOK AT THE WORLD AND TO TRY TO REALLY UNDERSTAND WHY WE EXIST...
THAT'S A HUGELY UPLIFTING FEELING!
THAT REALLY DOES GIVE A SENSE OF WORTH TO LIFE!

DAWKINS NOTES THAT WE SHOULD NOT BE SO *LAZY*, SO *DEFEATIST* AND *COWARDLY* AS TO SAY:

I DON'T UNDERSTAND IT SO IT MUST BE A *MIRACLE* — IT MUST BE *SUPERNATURAL* — *GOD DID IT!*

BETTER TO SAY INSTEAD:

WELL, IT'S *STRANGE*, IT'S A *PUZZLE* — BUT IT'S A *CHALLENGE* THAT WE SHOULD *RISE TO!*

WHETHER WE RISE TO THE CHALLENGE BY QUESTIONING THE TRUTH OF THE OBSERVATION, OR BY EXPANDING OUR SCIENCE IN NEW AND EXCITING DIRECTIONS — THE PROPER AND BRAVE RESPONSE TO ANY SUCH CHALLENGE IS TO *TACKLE IT HEAD-ON.*

AND UNTIL WE'VE FOUND A PROPER ANSWER TO THE MYSTERY, IT'S PERFECTLY OK SIMPLY TO SAY:

MIRACLES, MAGIC AND MYTHS, THEY CAN BE FUN. EVERYBODY LIKES A GOOD STORY! AS LONG AS YOU DON'T CONFUSE THEM WITH *THE TRUTH*!

THE *REAL* TRUTH HAS A MAGIC OF ITS OWN! THE TRUTH IS *MORE* MAGICAL, IN THE *BEST* AND *MOST EXCITING* SENSE OF THE WORD, THAN *ANY* MYTH OR MADE-UP MYSTERY OR MIRACLE!

SCIENCE HAS ITS *OWN* MAGIC – THE MAGIC OF *REALITY*!

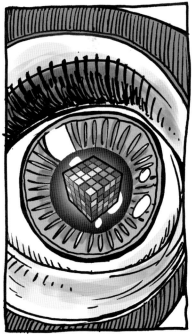

AS TO **ATHEISM**, HERE'S **SAM HARRIS** PUTTING IT PITHILY:

> 'ATHEISM' IS A TERM THAT SHOULD NOT EVEN **EXIST!**
>
> NO-ONE EVER NEEDS TO IDENTIFY HIM OR HERSELF AS A **'NON-ASTROLOGER'** OR A **'NON-ALCHEMIST'.**

ATHEISM IS NOTHING MORE THAN THE **NOISES** REASONABLE PEOPLE MAKE IN THE PRESENCE OF UNJUSTIFIED RELIGIOUS BELIEFS.

BUT SOMETIMES PEOPLE ASK: HOW DO WE APPRECIATE THINGS LIKE **MUSIC** AND THE BEAUTY OF **CHURCHES** WITHOUT BELIEVING IN GOD? OR HOW CAN WE FEEL **LOVE** IF WE DON'T LOVE GOD?

WELL, QUITE EASILY. VARIOUS GREAT WORKS MAY HAVE BEEN INSPIRED BY GOD, LIKE THE SISTINE CHAPEL...

...OR THE 1808 POEM BY WILLIAM BLAKE AND THE 1916 ANTHEM **'JERUSALEM'**, BY SIR HUBERT PARRY...

...OR ST MARK'S BASILICA IN VENICE.

> AND DID THOSE FEET IN ANCIENT TIME WALK UPON ENGLAND'S MOUNTAINS GREEN AND WAS THE HOLY LAMB OF GOD, ON ENGLAND'S PLEASANT PASTURES SEEN?

THIS IS AN IRONIC EXAMPLE, WHICH RATHER PROVES OUR POINT – ALTHOUGH PARRY'S ANTHEM IS OFTEN SUNG AS A HYMN, BLAKE'S ORIGINAL POEM IS NOT ABOUT GOD BUT ABOUT REVOLUTION.

ALL THESE AND MORE WONDERFUL WORKS OF ART MAY HAVE BEEN INSPIRED BY A BELIEF IN GOD (OR, MORE CORRECTLY, MANY OF THEM WERE MADE AS COMMISSIONS FROM RELIGIOUS AUTHORITIES).

BUT SUCH A BELIEF IS NOT NECESSARY IN ORDER TO ENJOY THE BEAUTY THAT SUCH WORKS OF ART HAVE IN THEIR OWN RIGHT. MILLIONS OF PEOPLE VISIT BEAUTIFUL CHURCHES LIKE ST MARK'S BASILICA, IN VENICE, AND MANY OF THEM WILL NOT BE CHRISTIANS OR BELIEVE IN ANY GOD AT ALL.

WELL WOULD'YA LOOK AT THAT!

ARE THE RELIGIOUS SAYING THAT **ONLY PRACTICING CHRISTIANS** CAN REALLY SEE THE BEAUTY OF THAT BUILDING?

ONLY **THEY** CAN **REALLY GRASP** THE INTRICACY OF THE CAREFULLY CRAFTED DETAILS?

ONLY *TRUE BELIEVERS* CAN FEEL A SENSE OF GRANDEUR
WHILE STANDING UNDER ITS ARCHES?

REALLY??

OR THAT *ONLY* THE RELIGIOUS CAN FEEL THEIR LUNGS AND THROAT FILL WITH JOY WHEN BELTING OUT A MOVING SONG?

ONLY THE RELIGIOUS CAN FEEL INSPIRED TO CREATE POETRY, PAINTINGS, YES, EVEN COMICS!?!

AND *ONLY* THE RELIGIOUS CAN FEEL *LOVE*?

IT'S A CLEAR AND EASILY VERIFIABLE *FACT* THAT HUMANISTS AND ATHEISTS *DO* FALL IN LOVE... AND EVEN THE BOOK YOU HOLD IN YOUR HAND IS AN INDICATION THAT THEY CAN ALSO MAKE AND APPRECIATE ART.

CHRISTOPHER HITCHENS NOTED ABOVE THAT RELIGIOUS FOLK DON'T SEEM TO BE MADE *HAPPY* BY THEIR FAITH. BUT THERE IS A *DIFFERENT* GROUP OF PEOPLE WHO *DO* SEEM TO BE MADE HAPPY BY WHAT THEY THINK AND PRACTICE:

PHYSICISTS!

HAVE YOU EVER SEEN A BUNCH OF MORE EXCITED BIG KIDS?

WHEN THEY ARE TALKING ABOUT THE LATEST DEVELOPMENT IN *ASTROPHYSICS* OR *SUB-ATOMIC PARTICLES* OR WHATEVER... THEY LOOK LIKE KIDS WITH A NEW TOY!

electron
atom
nucleus
neutron
proton
n p
gluon
up quark
down quark
Elizabeth Morales

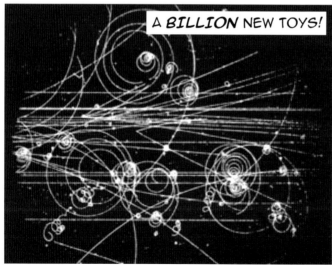

A *BILLION* NEW TOYS!

THAT *JOY* AND *ENTHUSIAM* YOU SEE ON THEIR FACES IS *CLEAR* AND *CATCHING*. THAT IS ONE EXAMPLE OF THE *MAGIC OF SCIENCE*.

ANOTHER IDEA COMMONLY ADVANCED BY RELIGIOUS PEOPLE IS THAT GOD IS A TYPE OF ***SOLACE***, A ***COMFORT*** IN THIS DIFFICULT WORLD.

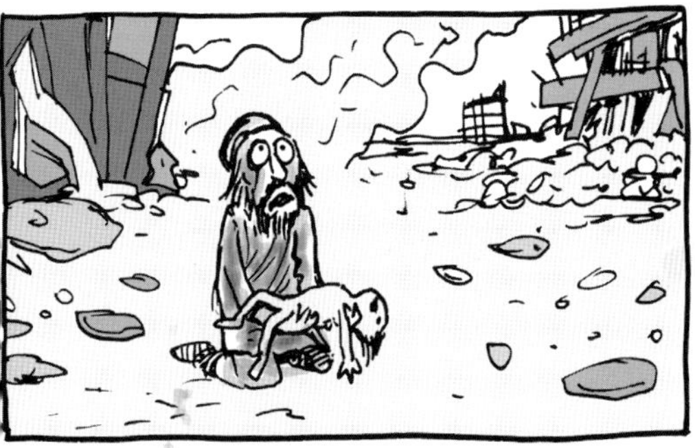

THIS IS THE IDEA OF A ***GOD*** OF ***LOVE***. SOMEONE WHO ***LOVES US*** UNCONDITIONALLY.

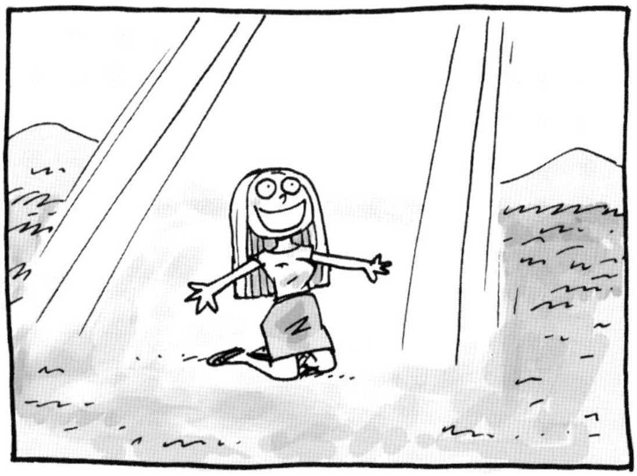

THIS MAY SOUND ***GOOD***. IT MAY MAKE US FEEL BETTER. AND SOME WHO ARE ***AGNOSTIC*** ABOUT GOD'S EXISTENCE SAY THEY WISH IT ***WERE*** TRUE.

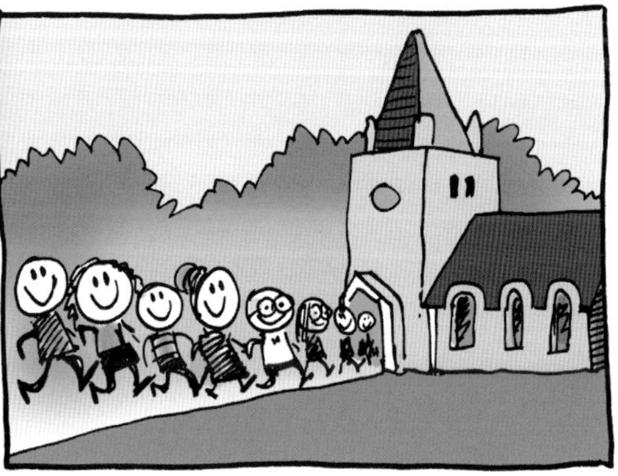

BUT OTHERS ***DISAGREE*** AND SAY THAT IT'S AN ***ACTIVELY GOOD*** THING TO THINK THAT THERE IS PROBABLY NO GOD. BECAUSE, IF THERE WERE, IT WOULD BE A ***TOTALITARIAN SLAVE SYSTEM!***

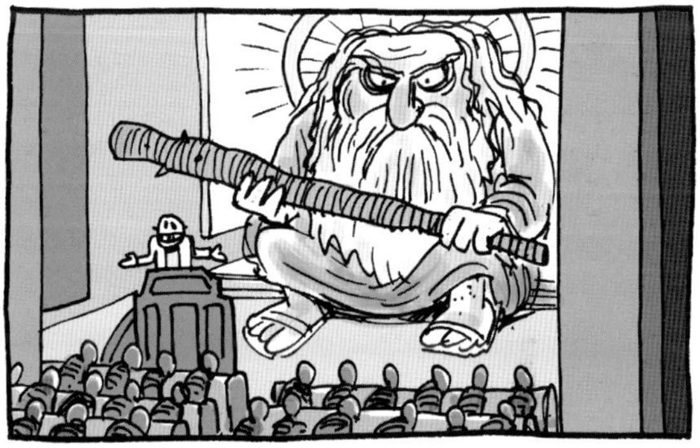

THEY ARGUE THAT WE WOULD BE ***SLAVES*** TO AN UNCHALLENGEABLE AUTHORITY WHOSE ***POWER*** OVER US CONTINUES ***AFTER*** WE ***DIE***. THEY ASK ***WHY***, IF THERE ***WERE*** A LOVING OR JUST GOD, HE SHOULD INSIST ON BEING ***ENDLESSLY*** AND ***BLINDLY WORSHIPPED***.

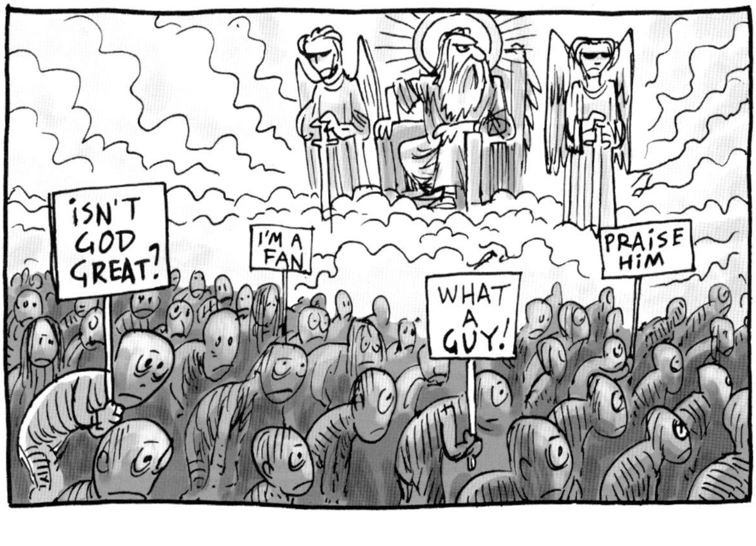
ISN'T GOD GREAT?
I'M A FAN
WHAT A GUY!
PRAISE HIM

HERE'S PHILOSOPHER **AC GRAYLING** NOW, WITH SOME IMPORTANT POINTS ABOUT WHAT HUMANISTS AND ATHEISTS THINK:

*HUMANISM IS **NOT** A RELIGIOUS BELIEF. OUR PRINCIPLES ARE **NOT** A FAITH.*

*WE DON'T RELY UPON SCIENCE AND REASON ALONE, THIS IS BECAUSE THEY ARE **NECESSARY** RATHER THAN **SUFFICIENT** FACTORS... BUT WE DISTRUST ANYTHING THAT CONTRADICTS SCIENCE OR REASON.*

*WHAT WE RESPECT IS **FREE INQUIRY**, **OPEN-MINDEDNESS**, AND THE **PURSUIT** OF IDEAS FOR THEIR OWN SAKE.*

*SOMETHING **SADLY LACKING** IN MANY RELIGIOUS PEOPLE.*

A QUESTION OFTEN ASKED IS 'IF YOU HAVE NO **GOD** THEN **WHERE** DO YOU GET YOUR **MORALS** FROM?'

ACCORDING TO THE BIBLICAL STORY, MOSES ASCENDED MOUNT SINAI AND, AFTER 40 DAYS AND NIGHTS, RECEIVED THE TEN COMMANDMENTS.

SO, DOES THIS MEAN THAT THE JEWISH PEOPLE, UNTIL THEY GOT TO MOUNT SINAI, HAD BEEN UNDER THE IMPRESSION THAT ADULTERY, MURDER, THEFT ETC ARE **OK**?...'

THEN, TO THEIR SURPRISE THEY FIND OUT FROM *MOUNT SINAI* THAT SUCH BEHAVIOR IS *NOT* SO GREAT AFTER ALL!

THE IMPLICATION OF THE STORY SEEMS TO BE THAT WE WOULD HAVE NO MORAL COMPASS IF WE WERE *NOT* UNDER THE STERN DICTATES OF A CELESTIAL AUTHORITY! HOW DOES THAT SQUARE WITH THE IDEALS OF *FREEDOM* AND THE *VALUE* OF THE *INDIVIDUAL*, OR WITH *DEMOCRACY*?

WHAT AN *INSULT* TO OUR DIGNITY AND INTELLIGENCE AS HUMANS! NO, IF WE HUMANS HAD *REALLY* THOUGHT ALL THOSE THINGS WERE OKAY WE WOULD NEVER HAVE MADE IT AS FAR AS MOUNT SINAI – WE WOULD HAVE KILLED OURSELVES OFF LONG BEFORE!

HUMAN DECENCY IS NOT *DERIVED* FROM RELIGION – IT *PRECEDES* IT. *MORALITY* IS PROBABLY INNATE AND *SOLIDARITY* IS PART OF OUR *SELF-INTEREST*, BOTH IN *SOCIETY* AND BETWEEN *INDIVIDUALS*.

HITCHENS LAID OUT A CHALLENGE TO US ALL REGARDING THIS QUESTION OF MORALS AND ETHICS...

CAN YOU NAME *ONE* ETHICAL STATEMENT MADE, OR *ONE* ETHICAL ACTION PERFORMED, BY A BELIEVER THAT COULD *NOT* HAVE BEEN UTTERED OR DONE BY A NONBELIEVER?

AND A *SECOND* CHALLENGE: CAN ANYONE THINK OF A *WICKED STATEMENT* MADE, OR AN *EVIL ACTION* PERFORMED, PRECISELY BECAUSE OF RELIGIOUS FAITH?

THE SECOND QUESTION IS EASY TO ANSWER, YES?

AS TO THE *FIRST*, THOUGH I'VE BEEN ASKING IT FOR *SOME TIME*, I'M STILL WAITING FOR A CONVINCING REPLY...

"RELIGION IS AN INSULT TO HUMAN DIGNITY. WITHOUT IT YOU WOULD HAVE GOOD PEOPLE DOING GOOD THINGS AND EVIL PEOPLE DOING EVIL THINGS. BUT FOR GOOD PEOPLE TO DO EVIL THINGS, THAT TAKES RELIGION." – STEVEN WEINBERG.

ANOTHER POINT HITCHENS BRINGS UP IS THAT OF THE CONCEPTION OF GOD AS BEING LIKE A *'CELESTIAL DICTATORSHIP'.*

HE SAID OF THIS:
'I DON'T HAVE ANY DESIRE TO LIVE UNDER A PERMANENT, UNALTERABLE DICTATORSHIP IN WHICH I HAVE NO SAY IN ITS CHOOSING! I DON'T WISH IT WAS TRUE THAT I COULD BE CONVICTED OF THOUGHT CRIME FOR WHAT I WAS THINKING WHEN I WAS ASLEEP!'

'LET ALONE FOR WHAT I WAS THINKING WHEN I WAS AWAKE!'

'WHEN I WAS IN SCHOOL I USED TO WONDER WHAT HEAVEN WOULD BE LIKE IF IT REALLY CONSISTED OF EVERLASTING PRAISE... SOUNDED LIKE HELL TO ME.'

'AND I THINK I SAW AN APPROXIMATION OF WHAT THAT WOULD BE LIKE WHEN I VISITED NORTH KOREA, IN WHICH IT IS THE DUTY AND JOB OF EVERY PERSON TO SPEND AN ETERNITY PRAISING THE DIVINE LEADER AND HIS DIVINE FATHER.'

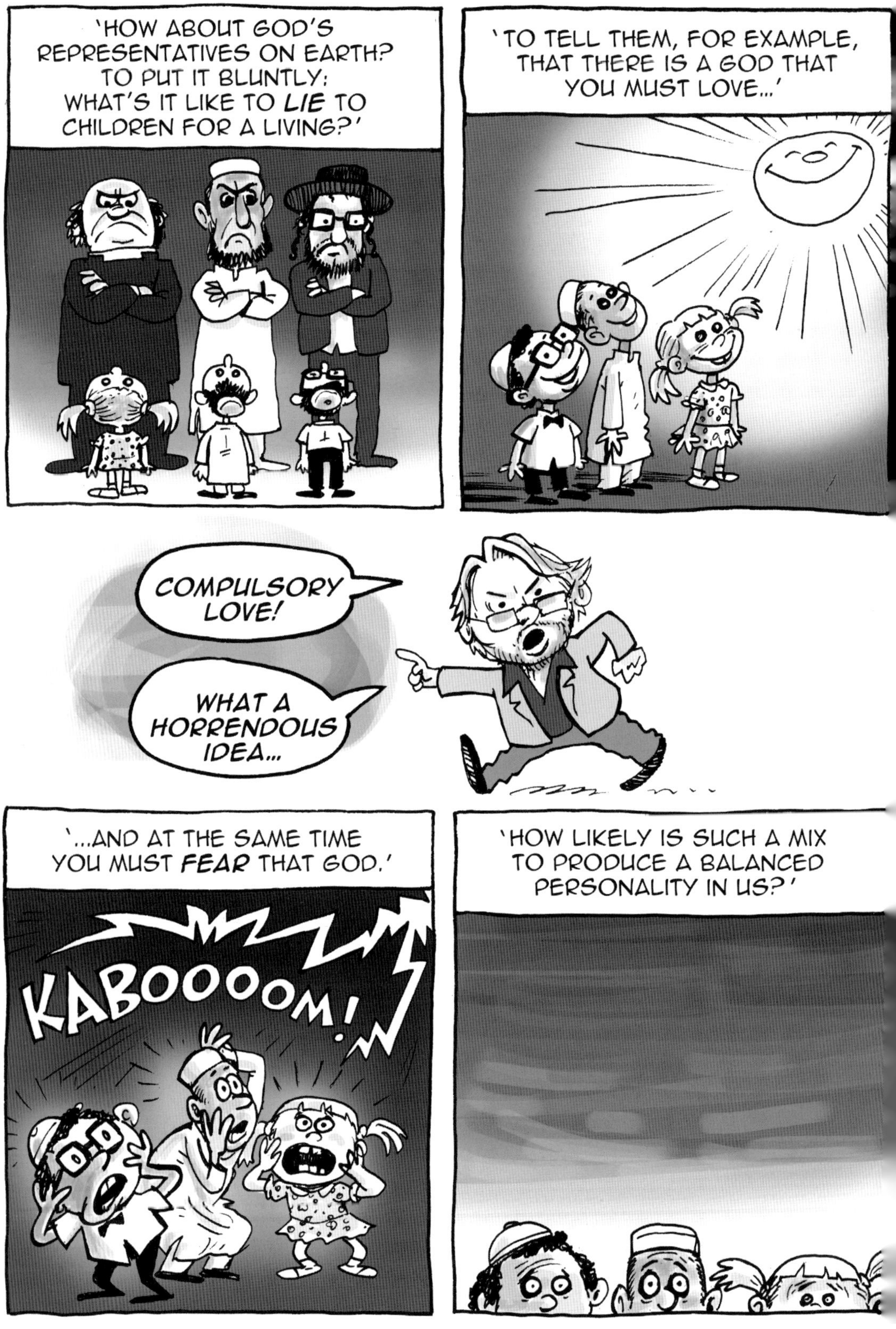
'HOW ABOUT GOD'S REPRESENTATIVES ON EARTH? TO PUT IT BLUNTLY: WHAT'S IT LIKE TO *LIE* TO CHILDREN FOR A LIVING?'
'TO TELL THEM, FOR EXAMPLE, THAT THERE IS A GOD THAT YOU MUST LOVE...'
COMPULSORY LOVE!
WHAT A HORRENDOUS IDEA...
'...AND AT THE SAME TIME YOU MUST *FEAR* THAT GOD.'
KABOOOOM!
'HOW LIKELY IS SUCH A MIX TO PRODUCE A BALANCED PERSONALITY IN US?'

HERE'S A **MOVING EFFORT** TO ENCOURAGE A HEALTHY BALANCE. *RICHARD DAWKINS'* LETTER TO HIS DAUGHTER...

To my dearest daughter,
Now that you are ten, I
want to write to you about
something that is important
to me.

'HAVE YOU EVER WONDERED HOW WE **KNOW** THE THINGS THAT WE KNOW? HOW DO WE **KNOW** THAT THE STARS, WHICH LOOK LIKE TINY PINPRICKS IN THE SKY, ARE REALLY HUGE BALLS OF FIRE LIKE THE SUN, AND VERY FAR AWAY?'

HE ANSWER IS **EVIDENCE.**

'SOMETIMES **EVIDENCE** MEANS ACTUALLY **SEEING, HEARING, FEELING, SMELLING...** THAT SOMETHING IS **TRUE.** ASTRONAUTS HAVE TRAVELED FAR ENOUGH FROM THE EARTH TO **SEE** THAT IT IS ROUND.'

SOMETIMES OUR YES NEED **HELP.** THE **"EVENING STAR"** LOOKS LIKE A BRIGHT TWINKLE IN THE SKY BUT WITH A TELESCOPE YOU CAN SEE THAT IT IS A BEAUTIFUL BALL – THE PLANET WE CALL **VENUS.'**

SOMETHING THAT YOU LEARN BY DIRECT SEEING IS CALLED AN OBSERVATION.'

DAWKINS GOES ON TO MENTION THREE BAD REASONS FOR BELIEVING IN ANYTHING: **TRADITION**, **AUTHORITY** AND **REVELATION**.

TRADITION MEANS BELIEFS HANDED DOWN FROM *GRANDPARENT* TO *PARENT* TO CHILD, OR FROM BOOKS HANDED DOWN OVER *CENTURIES*.

TRADITIONAL BELIEFS OFTEN START WITH SOMEBODY JUST *MAKING THEM UP*, LIKE THE STORIES ABOUT *THOR* AND *ZEUS*.

BUT AFTER *CENTURIES*, BEING SO *OLD* MAKES THEM SEEM *SPECIAL!* PEOPLE BELIEVE THINGS SIMPLY BECAUSE PEOPLE HAVE BELIEVED THE SAME THING BEFORE. THAT'S *TRADITION*.

THE TROUBLE WITH THAT IS... IF YOU *MAKE UP* A STORY THAT *ISN'T TRUE*, HANDING IT DOWN OVER CENTURIES DOESN'T MAKE IT ANY *TRUER!*

'*AUTHORITY*, AS A REASON FOR BELIEVING SOMETHING, MEANS *BELIEVING IT* BECAUSE YOU ARE *TOLD* TO BELIEVE IT BY SOMEBODY IMPORTANT. IN THE ROMAN CATHOLIC CHURCH, *THE POPE* IS THE MOST IMPORTANT PERSON, AND PEOPLE BELIEVE HE *MUST* BE RIGHT JUST BECAUSE HE *IS* THE POPE.'

'IN ONE BRANCH OF THE *MUSLIM* RELIGION, THE IMPORTANT PEOPLE ARE OLD MEN WITH BEARDS CALLED *AYATOLLAHS*. SOME YOUNG MUSLIMS ARE PREPARED TO COMMIT *MURDER*, PURELY BECAUSE THE AYATOLLAHS IN A FARAWAY COUNTRY TELL THEM TO.'

'THE *THIRD* BAD REASON FOR BELIEVING ANYTHING IS CALLED '*REVELATION*'... WHEN RELIGIOUS PEOPLE JUST HAVE A *FEELING* INSIDE THEMSELVES THAT SOMETHING MUST BE TRUE, EVEN THOUGH THERE IS *NO EVIDENCE* THAT IT *IS* TRUE, THEY CALL THEIR FEELING '*REVELATION*'... IT IS ONE OF THEIR MAIN REASONS FOR BELIEVING THE THINGS THAT THEY *DO* BELIEVE.'

BUT IS IT A *GOOD* REASON?

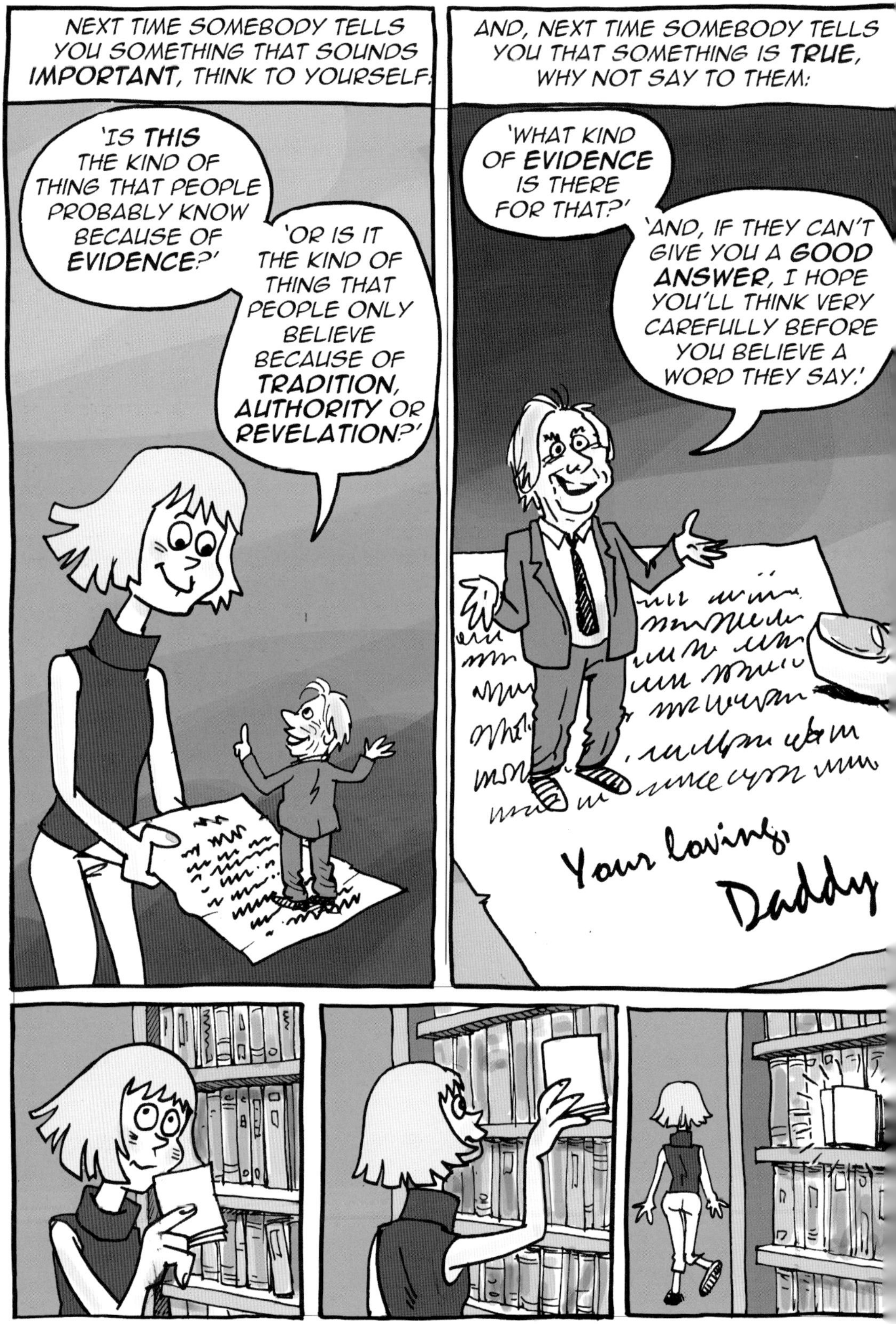
NEXT TIME SOMEBODY TELLS YOU SOMETHING THAT SOUNDS IMPORTANT, THINK TO YOURSELF:
'IS THIS THE KIND OF THING THAT PEOPLE PROBABLY KNOW BECAUSE OF EVIDENCE?'
'OR IS IT THE KIND OF THING THAT PEOPLE ONLY BELIEVE BECAUSE OF TRADITION, AUTHORITY OR REVELATION?'
AND, NEXT TIME SOMEBODY TELLS YOU THAT SOMETHING IS TRUE, WHY NOT SAY TO THEM:
'WHAT KIND OF EVIDENCE IS THERE FOR THAT?'
'AND, IF THEY CAN'T GIVE YOU A GOOD ANSWER, I HOPE YOU'LL THINK VERY CAREFULLY BEFORE YOU BELIEVE A WORD THEY SAY.'
Your loving, Daddy

UNFORTUNATELY, MANY PEOPLE *DON'T* ASK THE KIND OF QUESTIONS THAT *DAWKINS* ADVISES HIS DAUGHTER TO ASK. MANY PEOPLE STILL CONTINUE TO ACT ACCORDING TO *TRADITION*, *AUTHORITY* AND *REVELATION*, WITH NEGATIVE RESULTS FOR US ALL, SINCE THEIR ACTIONS OFTEN AFFECT OUR *EDUCATION, MEDIA, RELATIONSHIPS, HEALTH*, ETC.

TAKE *TRADITION*. OFTEN PEOPLE SAY SOMETHING LIKE:

THAT'S THE WAY WE DO THINGS HERE – IT'S *ALWAYS* BEEN DONE LIKE THAT!

BUT IS THAT A GOOD ENOUGH REASON, ON ITS OWN, FOR DOING ANYTHING... *REALLY?* JUST BECAUSE YOUR *GRANDMOTHER* AND YOUR *GRANDFATHER* DID IT, THEN *YOU* SHOULD TOO?

AFTER ALL, YOUR *GRANDPARENTS* USED TO HAVE AN *OUTSIDE TOILET* AND *NO HOT RUNNING WATER* WHEN THEY WERE KIDS! FANCY CONTINUING *THAT* HABIT, DO YOU?

AND YOUR *GREAT* GRANDPARENTS MAY WELL HAVE *ABUSED* AND *LOOKED DOWN ON* PEOPLE OF OTHER RACES... AND *THAT'S* ALRIGHT TOO, IS IT?

A GRAND OLD TRADITION WORTH KEEPING UP, HUH?!

ONE OF THE **NEGATIVE** CONSEQUENCES OF THIS BENDING THE KNEE TO AUTHORITY AND REVELATION IS THAT IT **REDUCES** OUR ABILITY OR TENDENCY TO **THINK** AND **DISCUSS**.

NULLIUS IN VERBA

"TAKE NOBODY'S WORD FOR IT", MOTTO OF THE ROYAL SOCIETY

WHAT IS THERE TO **THINK** ABOUT OR **DISCUSS** IF THE ANSWERS HAVE ALREADY BEEN REVEALED TO SOME WISE AUTHORITY?

AND... A CONNECTED POINT – IT OFTEN **DECREASES** OUR ABILITY TO BE **FLEXIBLE** AND **OPEN-MINDED!** OFTEN, OTHERWISE INTELLIGENT PEOPLE WILL **CLOSE OFF** FROM DISCUSSING ANYTHING THEY FEEL THREATENS THEIR RELIGION... THEIR MINDS ARE **CLOSED** ON THAT TOPIC. THEY **DON'T WANT TO KNOW.**

YOU'RE A PHD ENGINEERING STUDENT, HAKIM – HOW CAN YOU EXPLORE THE SCIENCE OF ENGINEERING BUT BE **TOTALLY CLOSED OFF** TO DISCUSSING **RELIGION?**

JOHN, I **TOLD** YOU THAT I DON'T WANT TO TALK ABOUT THIS ANY MORE!

WELL, **WHY?** WE'RE JUST TWO ADULTS TALKING ABOUT AN **INTERESTING** SUBJECT – CAN'T WE DO THAT CALMLY?

NO! I DON'T WANT TO!

OFTEN THEY SEE IT AS AN ATTACK ON THEM, ON THEIR **PERSON** AND SENSE OF **SELF**, OR THEIR **GROUP** SO, THEY REFUSE TO ENGAGE AT ALL... WHAT ARE THEY AFRAID OF?

DARWIN ——→ FASCISM

HOW ABOUT THE OFTEN-MADE POINT THAT *ATHEISM* LEADS TO A TYPE OF *AMORAL FASCISM?* THAT, FOR EXAMPLE, THE *NAZIS* IMPLEMENTED THE IDEAS OF *DARWIN.*

ACTUALLY, DARWIN'S THOUGHT WAS *NOT* TAUGHT IN GERMANY. DARWINISM WAS *DERIDED* IN GERMANY ALONG WITH EVERY OTHER FORM OF *UNBELIEF.*

ALL THE GREAT MODERN ATHEISTS, *DARWIN,* *EINSTEIN* AND *FREUD,* WERE *DESPISED* BY *HITLER'S REGIME.*

FORTUNATELY THIS ALLOWED THE *ESCAPE* OF ALL THESE GREAT ATHEISTS, THINKERS AND MANY OTHERS, TO THE UNITED STATES, A COUNTRY WHERE CHURCH AND STATE ARE *SEPARATED.* *THERE* THEY WERE MADE WELCOME...

AS HITCHENS OFTEN PROCLAIMED, **IF** THE NAZI REGIME WAS **ATHEIST**, HOW IS IT THAT, IN THE FIRST CHAPTER OF **MEIN KAMPF**, HITLER SAYS THAT HE'S EXECUTING **GOD'S WILL** IN DESTROYING THE JEWISH PEOPLE?

HOW IS IT THAT THE **FÜHRER OATH**, WHICH EVERY OFFICER OF THE PARTY AND THE ARMY HAD TO TAKE, MAKING HITLER INTO A **MINOR GOD**, BEGINS:

I SWEAR IN THE NAME OF **ALMIGHTY GOD** MY LOYALTY TO THE **FÜHRER!**

HOW IS IT THAT THE FIRST TREATY MADE BY THE NAZI DICTATORSHIP WAS WITH THE **VATICAN** – EXCHANGING **POLITICAL** CONTROL OF GERMANY FOR **CATHOLIC** CONTROL OF GERMAN **EDUCATION?**

HOW IS IT THAT ON THE **BELT BUCKLE** OF EVERY NAZI SOLDIER IT SAYS:

GOTT MIT UNS = GOD WITH US.

HAPPY BIRTHDAY ADOLF

HOW IS IT THAT THE **CATHOLIC CHURCH** CELEBRATED THE **BIRTHDAY** OF THE FÜHRER **EVERY YEAR** UNTIL **DEMOCRACY** PUT AN END TO THIS HORRIBLE, QUASI-RELIGIOUS SYSTEM?

HOW ABOUT *STALIN*? SURELY *HE* WAS AN ATHEIST AND LOOK WHAT HAPPENED *THERE*! WELL, WRONG AGAIN, – HE, *TOO*, CUNNINGLY USED RELIGION

PICTURE THE SITUATION: YOU'RE *STALIN*. YOU'VE TAKEN OVER *RUSSIA*, AFTER BEING EDUCATED IN A *SEMINARY*, AND WHAT DO YOU FIND?

YOU FIND THAT UP TO *1917*, FOR HUNDREDS OF YEARS, MILLIONS OF RUSSIANS HAVE BEEN TOLD THAT THE HEAD OF STATE, THE *TSAR*, IS A *GOD*.

YOU SHOULDN'T BE IN THE *DICTATORSHIP* BUSINESS IF YOU CAN'T TAKE ADVANTAGE OF A *DEEP WELL* OF *CREDULITY* AND *SERVILITY* LIKE *THAT*!

SO WHAT DOES HE DO? *HERESY TRIALS*... *WITCH HUNTS*... *MIRACULOUS DISCOVERIES*... THE WORSHIP OF THE *LEADER* FROM WHOM *ALL BLESSINGS FLOW*!

THERE IS NO POINT IN THE **RELIGIOUS** SETTING UP "STRAW MEN" ARGUMENTS AND KNOCKING THEM DOWN. WHAT DOES IT ACHIEVE? WHAT THEY NEED TO DO IN ORDER TO DEAL WITH THE **REAL** IDEAS OF HUMANISTS IS RESPOND TO **THIS**, HITCHENS' UNANSWERED CHALLENGE:

NAME ME A STATE THAT ADOPTED THE TEACHINGS OF...

LUCRETIUS

AND *DEMOCRITUS...*

OF *GALILEO*

*YET IT MOVES

EPPUR SI MU⊙VE...

AND *SPINOZA....*

...OF *RUSSELL*

AND *DARWIN*...

...OF *JEFFERSON*

AND *THOMAS PAINE*...

IF WE MAKE **THOSE** WHAT WE TEACH OUR CHILDREN, **IF** WE MAKE THAT **SCIENTIFIC** AND **RATIONALISTIC HUMANISM** OUR TEACHING...

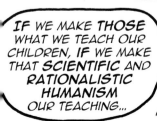

AND **IF** SUCH A STATE FELL INTO **TYRANNY** AND **FAMINE** AND **TORTURE**... THEN YOU WOULD **REALLY** HAVE SOMETHING TO ATTACK US ABOUT!

OWNERS OF **DOGS** WILL HAVE NOTICED THAT, IF YOU PROVIDE THEM WITH FOOD AND WATER AND SHELTER AND AFFECTION, THEY WILL THINK YOU ARE **GOD**...

WHEREAS OWNERS OF **CATS** ARE COMPELLED TO REALIZE THAT, IF YOU PROVIDE **THEM** WITH FOOD AND WATER AND SHELTER AND AFFECTION, THEY DRAW THE CONCLUSION THAT **THEY** ARE **GODS**.

THE GOVERNOR OF TEXAS WAS ASKED IF HE THOUGHT THE **BIBLE** SHOULD BE TAUGHT IN SCHOOLS IN **SPANISH**. HE REPLIED:

IF ENGLISH WAS GOOD ENOUGH FOR JESUS, THEN IT'S GOOD ENOUGH FOR ME.

HOW DID THE **AMISH GIRL** GET **EXCOMMUNICATED?**

TOO MENNONITE!
(BOOM BOOM)

RECENTLY WE HAVE SEEN THE **CHURCH OF ROME** BEFOULED BY ITS COMPLICITY WITH THE UNPARDONABLE SIN OF **CHILD RAPE**. OR, AS IT MIGHT BE PHRASED... "NO CHILD'S BEHIND LEFT."

SEAN FAIRCLOTH IS A FORMER *DEMOCRATIC MAJORITY WHIP* OF HIS LEGISLATURE, A LAWYER AND AUTHOR. AS AN *AGNOSTIC* HE CAME UP WITH 10 *PRACTICAL POINTS* FOR A *SECULAR AMERICA*. HE WANTS TO RETURN THE *US* TO THE ORIGINAL CONDITION OF *STATE-CHURCH SEPARATION*, SEEKING TO DO SO BY UNITING RELIGIOUS AND NON-RELIGIOUS PEOPLE IN THIS CAUSE.

1. RESPECT OUR TROOPS – OUR MILITARY SHALL SERVE AND INCLUDE *ALL* AMERICANS, RELIGIOUS OR NONRELIGIOUS, WITH NO HINT OF BIAS AND WITH NO HINT OF FUNDAMENTALIST EXTREMISM COLORING OUR MILITARY DECISIONS AT HOME OR ABROAD.

2. REPRODUCTIVE INFORMATION BASED ON SCIENCE – ANY FEDERAL OR STATE-FUNDED PROGRAM, WHETHER OFFERING SERVICES DOMESTIC OR FOREIGN, THAT RELATES TO REPRODUCTIVE DECISIONS SHALL BE BASED ON SCIENCE AND PUBLIC HEALTH; *NOT* ON RELIGIOUS BIAS, OR THE DENIGRATION OF WOMEN OR SECULAR MINORITIES.

3. HEALTHCARE PROFESSIONALS FULFILL PROFESSIONAL DUTIES – HEALTHCARE PROFESSIONALS SHALL FULFILL THEIR PROFESSIONAL DUTIES, AND THEY MUST DO SO WITHOUT A HINT OF RELIGIOUS BIAS OR THEY MUST FIND ANOTHER JOB. THAT INCLUDES FUNDAMENTALIST PHARMACISTS THAT TURN AWAY RAPE VICTIMS FROM PLAN-B (MORNING AFTER PILL EMERGENCY CONTRACEPTION).

4. NO RELIGIOUS BIAS IN LAND USE OR EMPLOYMENT – THERE SHALL BE NO BIAS IN LAND USE PLANNING OR ENVIRONMENTAL LAW OR EMPLOYMENT LAW BASED ON RELIGION OR LACK THEREOF.

5. NO BIAS IN MARRIAGE LAW – MARRIAGE CAN BE DEFINED BY RELIGIOUS CONGREGATIONS HOWSOEVER THEY CHOOSE WITHIN THEIR OWN SERVICES BUT MARRIAGE UNDER AMERICAN LAW SHALL HAVE NO BIAS WHATSOEVER.

6. AUTONOMY FOR END-OF-LIFE CHOICES – WHEN FACING END-OF-LIFE DECISIONS, ALL AMERICANS SHALL BE GUARANTEED CONTROL OVER THEIR OWN BODIES WITHOUT BEING THWARTED BY RELIGIOUS BIAS.

7. NO RELIGIOUS BIAS IN SCHOOL – AMERICA'S YOUTH SHALL NEVER BE SUBJECTED TO BIAS IN EDUCATION. IF THERE IS *ONE PENNY* OF GOVERNMENT FUNDS THERE CAN'T BE *ONE IOTA* OF RELIGIOUS BIAS.

8. CONGRESS SHALL INCLUDE SECULAR AMERICANS –
THE COMPOSITION OF CONGRESS AND LEGISLATURE SHALL INCLUDE SECULAR AMERICANS AND THERE SHALL BE NO BIAS AGAINST SECULAR CANDIDATES.

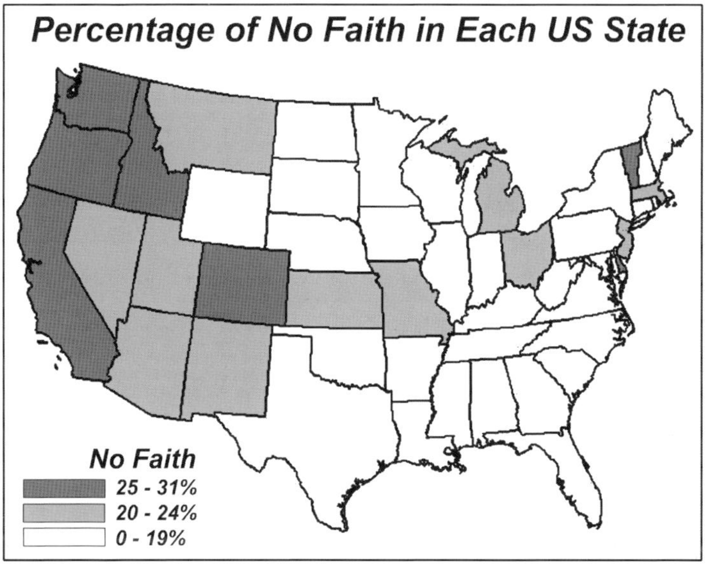
Percentage of No Faith in Each US State
No Faith
25 - 31%
20 - 24%
0 - 19%

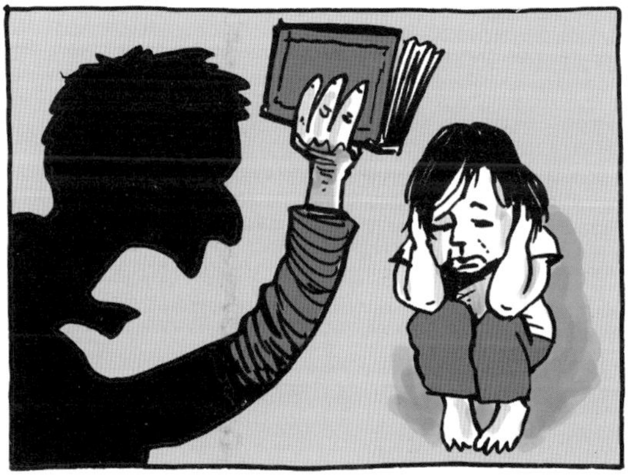

9. CHILDREN PROTECTED FROM RELIGIOUS ABUSE –
THERE SHOULD BE ONE CONSISTENT STANDARD PERTAINING TO THE HEALTH AND WELFARE OF CHILDREN, REGARDLESS OF A CHILD'S PARENTS, SCHOOL, OR CHILD CARE CENTER. THEY ARE ALL HUMAN BEINGS THAT DESERVE HUMAN RIGHTS AND PROTECTION.

10. MEDICAL & SCIENTIFIC INNOVATION SHALL BE DEDICATED TO HEALTH & ADVANCEMENT –
MEDICAL, TECHNICAL, AND SCIENCE INNOVATIONS SHALL BE DEDICATED TO THE HEALTH AND ADVANCEMENT OF OUR FELLOW CITIZENS AND MUST NEVER BE IMPEDED BY RELIGIOUS BIAS.

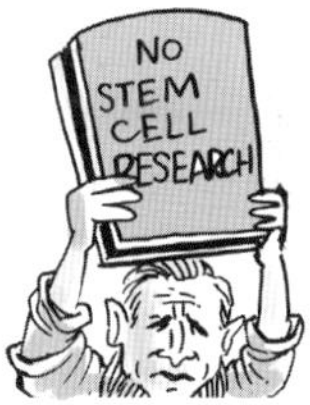
NO STEM CELL RESEARCH

IF ALL THESE GUIDELINES WERE KEPT TO IN MODERN AMERICA, IMAGINE WHAT A DIFFERENT COUNTRY IT WOULD BE!

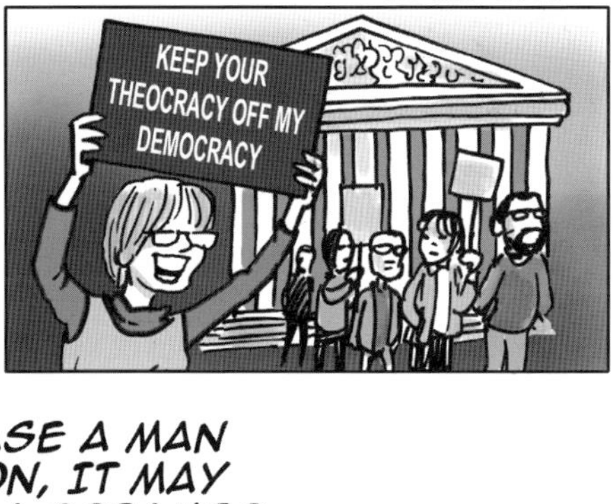
KEEP YOUR THEOCRACY OFF MY DEMOCRACY

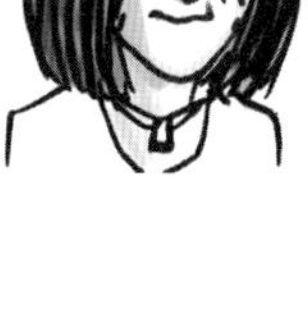

TO PARAPHRASE A MAN WITH A VISION, IT MAY SEEM LIKE I'M A DREAMER, BUT I'M NOT THE ONLY ONE...

MUCH IS MADE OF THE **CHRISTIAN** HERITAGE OF COUNTRIES LIKE THE **US** AND THE **UK**. **ANDREW COPSON**, THE CHIEF EXECUTIVE OF THE BRITISH HUMANIST ASSOCIATION, IS HERE TO SAY THAT WE SHOULD RECOGNIZE THE **SECULAR** INFLUENCE TOO:

FOR A START, **CHRISTIANS** OFTEN OPPOSED SOME OF THESE 'GOOD THINGS' IN THE PAST.

IN ADDITION, PRE-CHRISTIAN AND NON-CHRISTIAN SOCIETIES SEEM TO HAVE ACHIEVED *MANY* IF NOT *ALL* OF THESE ADVANCES AT VARIOUS TIMES *WITHOUT* THE SPUR OF A BELIEF IN JESUS.

GREAT ZEUS! DON'T LOOK UP. MEN - IT'S NOT A PRETTY SIGHT!

The Colossus of Rhodes

BUT MY SPECIFIC POINT IS THAT MEN AND WOMEN WITH HUMANIST VIEWS HAVE MADE A VERY LARGE CONTRIBUTION TO OUR NATIONAL LIFE AND SOCIETY.

HUMANIST ORGANIZATIONS IN THE 19TH CENTURY PIONEERED *HOUSING* AND *EDUCATION* PROJECTS AND, IN THE 20TH CENTURY, SUCH THINGS AS *NON-DIRECTIVE COUNSELLING* AND *ADOPTION AGENCIES*.

THIS WORK CONTINUES TODAY WITH HUMANIST PROJECTS IN AFRICA AND INDIA FOR EDUCATION AND THE RELIEF OF POVERTY, AND WITH THE PROVISION OF CEREMONIES SUCH AS FUNERALS, ATTENDED BY OVER 250,000 PEOPLE IN THE UK EACH YEAR AND MILLIONS WORLDWIDE.

KASESE HUMANIST PRIMARY SCHOOL

THIS WORK FOR THE COMMON GOOD IS SOMETHING WE SHOULD *ALL - HUMANIST* AND *NON-HUMANIST* - BE *PROUD* OF IN OUR *SHARED HISTORY!*

HUMANISTS WHO HAVE MADE SIGNIFICANT CONTRIBUTIONS TO SCIENTIFIC, INTELLECTUAL, ARTISTIC AND LITERARY HERITAGE INCLUDE:

EM FORSTER, NOVELIST.

BARBARA EHRENREICH, AN AMERICAN WRITER.

JOHN STUART MILL, THE FATHER OF MODERN LIBERALISM.

KATHARINE HEPBURN, ACTRESS.

AND ALSO: CHARLES DARWIN, RICHARD DAWKINS, DAVID KING, JOHN DEWEY, R BUCKMINSTER FULLER, JOHN LENNON, BRIAN COX, THOMAS HARDY, JOHN FOWLES, A J AYER, KARL POPPER, ANISH KAPOOR, J ROBERT OPPENHEIMER, B F SKINNER... AND MANY MORE.

TO DRAW ALL THIS TO A CONCLUSION. ALL THE POINTS, QUESTIONS, SARCASM, ARGUMENTS, JOKES, THEORIES, AND BELIEFS IN THIS BOOK RELATE TO HOW WE WANT TO LIVE OUR LIVES, RUN OUR SOCIETIES AND ACT AS INDIVIDUALS.

DO WE CHOOSE TO DO SO WITH *CONCERN* FOR OUR SHARED HUMANITY, FOR WHAT *UNITES* US?

DO WE CHOOSE *RATIONAL* AND *LOGICAL* APPROACHES TO PROBLEMS

OR *WILD ASSUMPTIONS* WITH *NO PROOF?*

DO WE *QUESTION?*

OR DO WE *BLINDLY ACCEPT?*

OUR BASIC MESSAGE TO THOSE WHO FOLLOW A RELIGION IS PUT WELL BY PHILOSOPHER *SIMON BLACKBURN,* VICE PRESIDENT OF THE *BRITISH HUMANIST ASSOCIATION:*

HUMAN BEINGS NEED TO BEHAVE WELL IN *THIS* WORLD, AND *NOT* ANY OTHER!

The American Humanist Association

The American Humanist Association (AHA) strives to bring about a progressive society where being 'good without a god' is an accepted way to live life. Humanists build on reason, free from theism or other supernatural beliefs and add empathy, compassion, and a commitment to egalitarianism. We are advocates for the causes that naturally flow from these principles, and accomplish that advocacy through our defense of civil liberties and secular governance, by our legal, legislative and public activism as well as our outreach to the growing number of people without religious belief or preference.

Secular government

Supporting the constitutional standard of separation of church and state is a key priority of the AHA. Government endorsement of any particular religion is a direct violation of the Jeffersonian wall between church and state and the First Amendment, which states 'Congress shall make no law respecting an establishment of religion'.

We work through our advocacy department to defeat proposed laws and eliminate existing laws that infringe upon this heritage. The AHA's legal organization, the Appignani Humanist Legal Center, participates in litigation to defend the constitutional right of all citizens to a secular government. Those actions target religious or sectarian imagery and text in government buildings and public spaces, religious ceremonies or prayer in government events and proceedings, and the expenditure of tax dollars to support religious programs, organizations, monuments, or other displays that inherently discriminate against millions of Americans who do not believe in the represented religion.

Scientific integrity

The AHA considers the integrity of scientific knowledge to be essential to a humanist society. For that reason, we insist that scientific studies be the sole basis for public policy and education. Religious or sectarian doctrine is irrelevant and immaterial to discerning the best policy.

The AHA has forcefully argued these principles in opposition to attempts to revive creationism and abstinence-only sex education in public schools. The AHA has also fought to allow research on treatments for debilitating diseases using embryonic stem cells and against the bar on federal funding based on the assumption that the small cluster of cells has the potential to be a person.

Human rights for all

Global standards for human rights are the ultimate guarantors of these rights, and adherence to international institutions such as the International Criminal Court, the United Nations Universal Declaration of Human Rights, and other frameworks is essential to the enforcement of individuals' rights the world over.

The AHA strongly affirms the inherent right of all individuals to freely make choices that affect themselves and their person. Human rights ensuring justice, including the right to a fair and speedy trial by an independent judiciary, to habeas corpus, and to proportionate punishment, must be guaranteed to all. Capital punishment, prisoner abuse, extraordinary rendition, and interrogative and penal torture reflect an explicit disregard for standards of humane treatment.

Promoting peace

The pursuit of peaceful and non-violent strategies for resolving the world's most dire conflicts, which often result in genocide, war, and autocracy, is paramount for human coexistence and progress. Pre-emptive war, unilateral conflict, arms proliferation, terrorism and indiscriminate use of force all threaten the common bonds of humanity that we all share.

The AHA believes that cultural exchange, cooperation, peaceful conflict resolution, and diplomacy through multilateral institutions, such as the United Nations, are the most appropriate ways to respect human rights and make the world a safer place for all of its inhabitants. Accordingly, the United States should sign on to the International Criminal Court, abide by and help enforce international law, and push other countries to strengthen the rule of law in their own societies.

Women's rights

The AHA promotes equality for women and men in all sectors, at all times, in all countries. While great progress has been made domestically, inequality and violence against women is still prevalent in many sectors. Women continue to be treated as second-class citizens in some countries, and are often subject to pain, humiliation, mutilation, and even death for reasons such as adultery, childbirth out of wedlock, or driving a car, while men are rarely punished for the same 'offenses'.

The AHA condemns all forms of gender-based violence, restrictions on women's reproductive choices, legal, religious, and societal discrimination, and any attempts to reduce women to second-class citizen status. We continue to act in favor of eliminating the gender gap, including support for girls' education, individual rights, compensation and benefits, and access to economic and social resources both domestically and worldwide.

The AHA also supports every woman's unequivocal moral and legal right to autonomy over her own body and reproductive choices. Women's access to family planning, contraception, birth control, emergency contraception, and healthcare services and resources should therefore be unrestricted by the government or religious preferences of private third parties.

LGBTQ rights

The AHA supports the growing majority of people who reject the idea that LGBTQ individuals and families are second-class citizens, and we encourage legislative reform of their rights to marry, adopt children, and live free from intimidation and violence.

State and federal laws that prohibit LGBTQ Americans from seeking civil marriage licenses, adopting children, and participating in publicly funded organizations endanger the freedom of expression of personal sexual identity and must be eliminated immediately.

Civil rights in America

The AHA will continue to work tirelessly in cases where civil rights have been compromised by the government, as the erosion of our guaranteed civil rights is a great danger. Membership in the International Criminal Court would ensure that when the entire American system of justice fails, American political interests will not prevent rogue American leaders from being brought to justice.

Government discrimination based on race, heritage, class or religion undermines the universality of these rights. Racial profiling, official discrimination against minorities, government sponsorship and favor to religious groups, and unwarranted detentions threaten the tenets of our free, open, and pluralistic society.

Join the American Humanist Association at www.americanhumanist.org and follow the AHA on Facebook, Twitter, and other social media.

BRITISH HUMANIST ASSOCIATION

for the one life we have

The British Humanist Association

Have you heard of the British Humanist Association? We're the national charity working on behalf of non-religious people who seek to live ethical and fulfilling lives on the basis of reason and humanity.

Our mission is to promote Humanism – which is to say, living an ethical life on the basis of reason and humanity, without reference to religion – and we represent the non-religious in Britain, and support those who wish to live humanist lives, including through the provision of humanist ceremonies. We also offer a humanist perspective in public debate, drawing on contemporary humanist thought and the worldwide humanist tradition.

What we do

We campaign for the separation of church and state and for equal treatment in law and policy of everyone regardless of religion or belief, and campaign on public ethical issues such as abortion, marriage and assisted dying.

One of the main areas where we target our campaigning is education. A third of state-funded schools in England and Wales are religious in character, with most being Church of England or Roman Catholic, but a number also being Jewish, Methodist and, in more recent years, Muslim, Hindu, and Sikh. These schools are legally allowed to discriminate in terms of the pupils they admit and staff they employ, in favour of not just those of their own faith, but with respect to admissions, also those of other faiths to the detriment of those of no faith. All of these schools are fully or virtually fully state-funded. This is discriminatory and divisive and so we campaign against the state continuing to fund these schools. We employ the UK's only dedicated campaigner working against 'faith' schools.

It's a far cry from the situation in America, for example, where all state schools are required by the constitution to be secular.

We do not believe that there should be any proselytizing in schools so wish to see an end to faith-based RE, and the law requiring daily collective worship in all state schools repealed and replaced by another law requiring inclusive school assemblies. On the other hand, we think it's very important for young people to learn about different religions and non-religious worldviews, as understanding of such beliefs is vital in order to be able to understand each other and wider society. We think that should include teaching young people about Humanism as well.

Creationism in the United Kingdom

We've been at the forefront of battles in the UK to make sure evolution is taught in schools and ideas such as young earth creationism and intelligent design are not falsely presented as scientifically valid by schools and teachers.

Science education is hugely important and every young person deserves to be given a robust understanding of the scientific method, including an appreciation of how life came to be, but at some state-funded schools, pseudoscientific ideas continue to be peddled to impressionable young people. Because of this, we teamed up with leading science associations, some religious groups, and 30 prominent scientists in 2011 to launch the 'Teach evolution, not creationism!' campaign, which has been hugely successful.

One of the campaigns' aims was to get evolution taught at an earlier age, before age 11, rather than the previous law in England which said that evolution didn't have to be taught until pupils were 14. The consensus among scientists is that 14 is far too late to introduce such a central concept in biology.

Its other aim was to root out creationism and intelligent design from state-funded schools in the UK. At the time we launched the campaign, dozens of creationist groups were in the middle of applying to set up 'Free Schools', a new type of school in England which didn't have to adhere to the statutory curriculum or employ qualified teachers. This represented a terrifying prospect for the future of English education.

Over time, the campaign achieved success on all fronts, prompting the government to preclude Free Schools from 'teaching, as an evidence-based view or theory, of any view or theory that is contrary to established scientific and/or historical evidence and explanations' – i.e. no creationism as science. By 2014, it extended these rules to all UK schools, and in September of that year, it also introduced a new module on evolution to primary schools, marking a total victory for 'Teach evolution, not creationism!'

We'd like to say this is 'job done', and that creationism is now well and truly banished from UK schools, but sadly that isn't the case.

Ensuring science is taught properly in schools

Unfortunately, the threat of creationism is still alive in Britain, and it can take insidious forms. For example, the exam regulator was forced to announce in 2014 that censoring science exam questions was not allowed after a state-funded Jewish school in London was found to be blacking out questions on evolution, so as to insulate their pupils from having to learn about it!

And yet, despite this, in October the school in question got a 'Good' rating from the schools inspectorate, Ofsted, whose report didn't touch on the teaching of evolution or creationism at the school. As it is, Ofsted is not properly equipped to tackle the teaching of pseudoscience in the UK, and this is particularly the case in private schools, where all too often it is creationists carrying out the inspections themselves.

As a result, Ofsted is now the main focus of our campaigns around creationism and evolution – because it's vital that every young person receives a high-quality, broad and balanced education including in English, maths, the arts, the humanities and, of course, science.

You can find out more about our work, including how you can support it, by visiting www.humanism.org.uk.

About the author and illustrator

Sean Michael Wilson is a comic-book writer from Scotland, living in Japan. He has had many books published with a variety of US, UK and Japanese publishers, such as a graphic-novel version of *A Christmas Carol* ('Best of 2008', Sunday Times), *AX:alternative manga* ('Best ten books of 2010', Publishers Weekly), *Parecomic* (with an introduction by Noam Chomsky), and a manga version of the Japanese classic *The Book of Five Rings*. His books are often on themes of history, biography and social issues.
seanmichaelwilson.weebly.com

Hunt Emerson has drawn comics since the early 1970s, and has been featured in more publications than he can remember. He has published over 30 comic books of his own idiosyncratic stories, including reworkings of *Dante's Inferno*, *Casanova*, and *Lady Chatterley's Lover*. His strips currently appear in *The Beano*, *Fortean Times* magazine and *Fiesta*. In 2000 he was included in '75 Grand Masters of European Comics' by the renowned French comics institute the CNBDI. He lives in Birmingham, UK.
largecow.com

Related titles by New Internationalist

newint.org